DIABETES
Quick*flip*

Cookbook

Eileen Faughey, MA, RD

**American
Diabetes
Association.**

Director, Book Publishing, John Fedor; *Associate Director, Consumer Book Acquisitions,* Sherrye Landrum; *Editor,* Laurie Guffey; *Production Manager,* Peggy M. Rote; *Book Design,* Studio Signorella; *Composition,* Circle Graphics, Inc.; *Photography,* Russell McDougal; *Food Stylist,* Mary Taylor; *Cover Design,* VC Graphics, Inc.; *Printer,* Transcontinental, Inc.

Printed in Canada
1 3 5 7 9 10 8 6 4 2

The suggestions and information contained in this publication are generally consistent with the *Clinical Practice Recommendations* and other policies of the American Diabetes Association, but they do not represent the policy or position of the Association or any of its boards or committees. Reasonable steps have been taken to ensure the accuracy of the information presented. However, the American Diabetes Association cannot ensure the safety or efficacy of any product or service described in this publication. Individuals are advised to consult a physician or other appropriate health care professional before undertaking any diet or exercise program or taking any medication referred to in this publication. Professionals must use and apply their own professional judgment, experience, and training and should not rely solely on the information contained in this publication before prescribing any diet, exercise, or medication. The American Diabetes Association—its officers, directors, employees, volunteers, members, and the author—assume no responsibility or liability for personal or other injury, loss, or damage that may result from the suggestions or information in this publication.

♾ The paper in this publication meets the requirements of the ANSI Standard Z39.48-1992 (permanence of paper).

ADA titles may be purchased for business or promotional use or for special sales. For information, please write to Lee Romano Sequeira, Special Sales & Promotions, at the address below.

American Diabetes Association
1701 North Beauregard Street
Alexandria, VA 22311

Library of Congress Cataloging-in-Publication Data

Faughey, Eileen.
      Diabetic quickflip to delicious dinners / Eileen Faughey.
         p. cm.
      ISBN 1-58040-057-4 (pbk. : alk. paper)
      1. Diabetes–Diet therapy–Recipes. I. Title.

   RC662 .F38 2001
   641.5'6314–dc21

                   2001022390

Contents

Mexican Oven-Baked Dish

"I want to eat healthier meals, but I need new ideas for what to make."

"I want to prepare healthier meals, but I don't have the time."

After hearing comments like these over and over from people I counsel in my nutrition practice, I realized that we need more than nutrition facts to improve our eating habits. We need tools that will help us bridge the gap between what we know we should be eating and what we actually eat. As a Registered Dietitian with training at the Culinary Institute of America, I wanted to make it easy and convenient for people to prepare nutritious, good-tasting meals.

The *Diabetes* **Quick***flip* *Cookbook* does this by removing the clutter and confusion of countless recipes and organizing them into a simple, logical system. I hope you'll enjoy and benefit from the **Quick***flip*.

Eileen Faughey

A Note about Food Labels

Many food labels in the grocery store use terms that can be confusing. To help you shop and eat better, here is a list of the common terms as defined by the Food and Drug Administration.

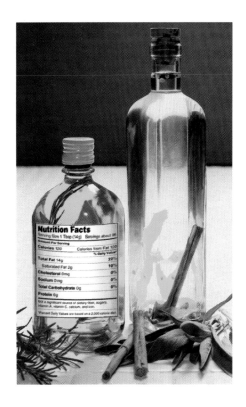

Fat

Fat Free, Nonfat: Less than 0.5 gram of fat per serving.

Low Fat: 3 grams or less of fat per serving. (If servings are smaller than 30 grams, or smaller than 2 tablespoons, this means 3 grams or less of fat per 50 grams of food.)

Reduced Fat, Less Fat: At least 25% less fat per serving than the regular product.

Sugar

Sugar Free: Less than 0.5 gram of sugar per serving.

No Added Sugar, Without Added Sugar, No Sugar Added: This does not mean the same as "sugar free." A label bearing these words means that no sugars were added during processing, or that processing does not increase the sugar content above the amount the ingredients naturally contain. Consult the nutrition information panel to see the total amount of sugar in this product.

Reduced Sugar: At least 25% less sugar per serving than the regular product.

Calories

Calorie Free: Fewer than 5 calories per serving.

Low Calorie: 40 calories or less per serving. (If servings are smaller than 30 grams, or smaller than 2 tablespoons, this means 40 calories or less per 50 grams of food.)

Reduced Calorie, Fewer Calories: At least 25% fewer calories per serving than the regular product.

Cholesterol

Cholesterol Free: Less than 2 milligrams of cholesterol, and 2 grams or less of saturated fat per serving.

Low Cholesterol: 20 milligrams or less of cholesterol, and 2 grams or less of saturated fat per serving.

Reduced Cholesterol, Less Cholesterol: At least 25% less cholesterol, and 2 grams or less of saturated fat per serving than the regular product.

Sodium

Sodium Free: Less than 5 milligrams of sodium per serving.

Low Sodium: 140 milligrams or less of sodium per serving.

Very Low Sodium: 35 milligrams or less of sodium per serving.

Reduced Sodium, Less Sodium: At least 25% less sodium per serving than the regular product.

Meat and Poultry

Foods that are labeled **"Light"** or "Lite" are usually either lower in fat or lower in calories than the regular product. Some products may also be lower in sodium. Check the nutrition information label on the back of the product to make sure.

Light or Lite Foods

Lean: Less than 10 grams of fat, 4.5 grams or less of saturated fat, and less than 95 milligrams of cholesterol per serving and per 100 grams.

Extra Lean: Less than 5 grams of fat, less than 2 grams of saturated fat, and less than 95 milligrams of cholesterol per serving and per 100 grams.

How to Use the Quick*flip*™

French Salmon, Southwestern Quinoa

Discover an innovative

system that lets you turn

a basic recipe into

5 delicious variations—

simply by changing a few

ingredients.

The *Diabetes* **Quick***flip* *Cookbook* was designed to simplify meal preparation. First stock your **Pantry** with the items listed on page 5. Next, select a recipe and decide which variation you would like to prepare. Now, all you need to prepare that recipe are the fresh ingredients. These are shown in green—that's your **Shopping List** for that meal.

Each recipe has **Cooking Directions** at the top of the page. This one set of instructions is used to make each of the **International Variations** of that recipe. On the page before the recipe, you will find some **Tips and Hints** for preparing the recipes in that group.

There is an additional **Guide to Choosing Ingredients** on page 36, as well as **Nutrition Facts** and **Food Exchange** information on page 37. Feel free to adjust the recipes to your own personal taste. This is a system that encourages you to be creative.

It's as simple as that. You're on your way to good eating.

The **Quick**_flip_™ _Flavors_ healthy ingredients from _around_ the world

The **Quick**_flip_ uses a wide variety of wholesome ingredients from this global pantry. Recipes emphasize plant foods, including grains, fruits, vegetables, beans, nuts, and herbs and spices. In addition to containing vitamins, minerals, and fiber, these foods are rich sources of health-promoting phytochemicals. They also offer a wonderful array of flavors, colors and textures.

When you think of a healthy diet, do you think of bland, tasteless food and a long list of all the delicious foods you shouldn't eat? Fortunately, with our better understanding of nutrition today, you no longer have to think that way. Today's nutritional guidelines are not based on narrow food choices and "dieting," but on enjoying a wide variety of delicious healthy foods in moderation.

The "new" nutritional guidelines are actually not new at all. They are based on traditional diets from around the world that we now know are linked with good health. The world's cuisines are rich in flavors and healthy ingredients. Adding these healthy foods may be just as important, if not more so, than limiting the foods we shouldn't eat.

The Quick_flip_ recipes incorporate the best of diets from around the world and use common, easy to find ingredients that are combined in creative ways. Many of the recipes use vegetables generously—even as a flavoring for rice dishes. Fruits and nuts are used to make appetizing desserts.

The Quick_flip_ recipes include protein sources such as chicken and fish in the smaller amounts recommended for good health or they are optional. The recipes give you the flexibility to make vegetarian dishes or to increase, decrease, add or delete ingredients to your personal taste.

Since the type of fat we eat may be more important for good health than how much fat we eat, the Quick_flip_ recipes use healthy sources of fat such as olive oil and nuts in moderate amounts.

As you flip through the Quick_flip's_ recipe pages you'll quickly see that a healthy diet is not one that restricts and limits foods. Instead, it's one that expands the choices and adds variety, nutrients and flavor.

Perhaps the best thing about using the Quick_flip_ is that it makes it easy to prepare healthy meals. You'll have more time to relax and enjoy what you eat—another important part of a healthy lifestyle!

The *Pantry*

A thoughtfully stocked pantry is the backbone of the kitchen.

This pantry list was devised for these recipes, but you'll find it helpful for making many other meals. Pantry items are listed in **purple** in each recipe. Ingredients that are best purchased fresh are listed in **green**.

Feel free to substitute items that you have on hand and increase or decrease the measure of ingredients to suit your own tastes. The **Quick***flip*™ system invites you to try new combinations.

Canned Goods

Apple juice concentrate
Artichoke hearts
Beans—black, garbanzo,
   pinto, refried,
   cannellini (or dried
   beans)
Broth—vegetable or
   chicken (or home
   made)
Evaporated skim milk
Green chilies
Mandarin oranges
Pineapple tidbits
Tomatoes
Tomato juice
Tomato paste
Tomato puree
Tomato sauce
Tuna
Water chestnuts
Yams

Dried/Frozen Fruits and Vegetables

Raisins
Sun-dried tomatoes
Frozen blackberries,
   blueberries,
   strawberries

Grains/Starches

Beans—see canned goods
Cornmeal
Lentils
Polenta (corn grits)
Couscous
Flour—if making your
   own pizza crust
Pasta—several varieties
   perhaps including:
   bow tie, fettuccine,
   lasagna, penne, shells,
   udon noodles, ziti
Quinoa
Rice—brown, white,
   basmati, jasmine

Nuts and Seeds

(These can be stored in airtight containers in the refrigerator or freezer)

Almonds
Peanuts
Pine nuts
Walnuts
Sesame seeds
Peanut butter
Tahini (ground sesame
   seeds)

Oils

Olive, dark sesame, canola

Vinegars

Balsamic, red wine, rice

Wines

Red and white

Spices, Flavorings, and Condiments

(The following items are used in the recipes, but you can edit this list to your liking.)

Allspice, almond flavor, basil, cayenne pepper, cardamom, chili powder, cinnamon, cloves, cocoa powder, coriander, cumin, curry, dill, garlic cloves, garlic powder, Italian herb seasoning, marjoram, nutmeg, oregano, pepper, red pepper flakes, salt, tarragon, thyme, turmeric

Cornstarch, honey, prepared mustard, mirin, olives, salsa, lite soy sauce or tamari, Thai chili paste, Thai fish sauce, Worcestershire sauce

Salads

Healthy HINTS

- Leafy greens are nutritional powerhouses. They contain beneficial antioxidants and phytochemicals in addition to the vitamins folate and riboflavin and the minerals magnesium, potassium, iron, and calcium.

- For variety, add roasted vegetables or cooked vegetables to salad greens or make a salad of vegetables other than greens. Try a cold salad of cooked vegetables with a low-fat Italian vinaigrette.

- Invest in good quality, flavorful ingredients such as a fruity olive oil, pungent balsamic vinegar, and flavorful Kalamata olives, and you can get by with half as much.

Tasty HINTS

- For a tasty change from iceberg lettuce, try peppery arugula, sharp watercress, or the mildly bitter Belgian endive or radicchio. The milder Bibb, Boston, and red and green leaf lettuces are also nice additions.

- Mesclun is a combination of tender greens such as arugula, radicchio, baby spinach, and dandelion. It is available in many supermarkets.

- Fruit, including kiwi, apples, pears, mandarin oranges, or pineapple chunks, adds variety and flavor to salads.

To lower fat in salad dressings:

- Use yogurt or tofu instead of oil, or substitute vegetable or chicken stock, juice, or water for all or some of the oil.
- Mix equal parts of regular salad dressing and vinegar or lemon juice.
- Use less acidic, milder tasting vinegars, such as balsamic, sherry, and rice vinegars that require less oil to balance the acidity.
- Add other ingredients such as mustard or pureed vegetables. This makes a vinaigrette dressing more creamy and less likely to separate, allows you to use less oil, and adds flavor.

Italian Salad

Helpful HINTS

- Add strips of grilled chicken or fish; seasoned, baked tofu; or cooked beans to your salad for added protein, texture, and flavor. Serve with bread and/or soup for a complete meal.

- Mix the salad dressing ahead of time so the flavors can blend more thoroughly. To keep the salad crisp, add the dressing just before serving.

Cooking Directions for the Basic Recipe

❶ Prepare the salad dressing. Mix the acidic liquid, seasonings, and base together. (For the French and Asian versions, mix the acidic liquid and seasoning in a small bowl or jar, add the oil and whisk or shake vigorously. For the Creamy Greek, Italian, and Middle Eastern versions, blend all the ingredients in a blender until smooth.)

❷ Prepare the salad greens, vegetables and fruits, and toppings (and grill or bake the salmon for the Italian version).

❸ Mix greens, vegetables, and fruits in a large bowl.

❹ Add salad dressing and topping and serve.

Five International Variations

Salads
4 to 5 Servings

Ingredients	ASIAN	FRENCH	GREEK	ITALIAN	MIDDLE EASTERN
Acidic Liquids	1/3 cup wine vinegar	1/2 cup **orange juice** 1/3 cup balsamic vinegar	2 T. wine vinegar 1 T. **lemon juice**	2 T. balsamic or red wine vinegar	2 T. fresh **lemon juice**
Seasonings		2 tsp. Dijon mustard 1/4 tsp. pepper	1 clove garlic 1/2 tsp. dried oregano 1/8 tsp. pepper salt, optional	1 small garlic clove 1/4 cup fresh **basil** 1/4 tsp. black pepper dash salt, optional	1 T. Dijon mustard 3/4 tsp. cumin 1/8 tsp. cinnamon, optional
Base	1 T. sesame oil 3 T. lite soy sauce	1/2 T. canola oil 2 tsp. toasted sesame oil	6 oz. **tofu**	2 large **tomatoes** 1 T. olive oil, optional	3/4 cup plain **yogurt**
Greens*	1 large or 2 small bunches **spinach**	1 large head Romaine lettuce 1 bunch **arugula**	1 large bunch **watercress** (or any greens)	1 large head **red leaf** lettuce 1 cup **mesclun**[h]	1 large head Romaine lettuce
Other Vegetables/ Fruit	1 can (8 oz.) water chestnuts, sliced 1 can (11 oz.) mandarin oranges (or fresh orange segments)	1 large **apple**, diced	1/2 cup sun-dried tomatoes** (or 1 cup fresh tomatoes, sliced) 14-oz. can artichoke hearts, drained and quartered	2 **tomatoes**, sliced 1/2 small **red onion**, very thinly sliced 3/4 cup **strawberries**, very thinly sliced	1 **cucumber**, diced 1/2 cup **scallions**, chopped 2 **tomatoes**, chopped
Topping	2 T. sliced almonds, toasted[†]	2 T. chopped walnuts, toasted[†]	2 T. pitted olives, chopped 2 T. crumbled **feta cheese**	2-oz. piece of grilled **salmon** for each salad 2 T. chopped walnuts, toasted[†]	1/2 cup fresh **parsley**, chopped 1/4 cup fresh **mint**, chopped

*Use the suggested greens or any salad greens of your choice. Plan for 1 1/2–2 cups leafy greens per person. Tear into bite-sized pieces.

**Rehydrated in 3/4 cup boiling water for 5 minutes and drained.

[h] See hints on the previous page.

[†] Toasting nuts: see hints on page 12.

Soups

Healthy
HINTS

- Soups are a delicious and easy way to get some of the 3–5 daily servings of vegetables recommended for good health.

- Pureeing all or part of the soup gives it a creamy texture without adding extra fat. Soups can also be thickened by adding a starch such as rice or potato or by adding evaporated skim milk.

- You can use a low-sodium broth to lessen the salt content and adjust the seasonings to your taste.

Tasty
HINTS

- The longer the soups cook, the more the flavors will blend and intensify.

- Add rice, noodles, or beans for a heartier version of the vegetable soup.

- Serve any of the soups with a crusty bread and salad for a complete meal.

Helpful
HINTS

- *To puree*: It's best to puree the soup in batches. Fill a blender about 1/3 full, wrap a dishtowel around the lid, start on a low speed and gradually increase the speed. Puree until smooth. You can also use a food processor.

- *Partial puree*: Pour half of the soup from your saucepan into a blender and puree until smooth. Return the pureed portion to the saucepan and stir.

- *To toast the bread:* Cut or tear a loaf of bread into small pieces. Toast in a 350° oven for 5–8 minutes until the bread is dry. Breadcrumbs may be substituted, if desired.

- Chop the vegetables into small pieces so they'll cook quickly. Add vegetables that take longer to cook, such as sweet potatoes and carrots, before adding quicker-cooking vegetables such as tomatoes.

Southwestern Yam Soup

Cooking Directions for the Basic Recipe

❶ Heat oil in a large (at least 4 qt.) saucepan.

❷ Add vegetables and cook for about 5 minutes over medium to medium-high heat.

❸ Add liquid, legumes if used, and seasonings.

❹ Simmer, covered, for 20 minutes over low heat* or until vegetables and legumes are cooked.

*For the Southwestern Yam soup, cook over medium heat for 20 minutes or until the yams are soft.

❺ Puree[h] all or part of the soup according to chart below.

Five International Variations

Soups
6 to 8 Servings

Ingredients	CALIFORNIAN VEGETABLE ⋯	INDIAN CURRIED LENTIL ⋯	MEDITERRANEAN ONION ⋯	MIDDLE EASTERN HUMMUS ⋯	SOUTHWESTERN YAM ⋯
Oil	1 T. olive oil	1 T. olive oil	1 T. olive oil	1 T. olive oil	1 T. canola or olive oil
Vegetables	1 cup **onion**, finely chopped 2 T. **garlic**, minced 1/2 cup **carrot**, finely chopped 1 cup **zucchini**, finely chopped 1/2 cup **celery**, chopped 14-oz. can diced tomatoes or 5 plum **tomatoes**, diced 1/4 cup tomato paste	1 cup **onion**, chopped 1/4 cup **carrots**, finely chopped 1/4 cup **celery**, chopped 2 T. fresh garlic, minced	5 cups **onions**, thinly sliced 2 T. **garlic**, minced	1 cup **onion**, chopped 4 T. garlic, minced 1/2 cup **carrot**, finely chopped 1 cup **celery**, chopped	4 medium **yams**, diced 1 cup **onions**, chopped 2 T. fresh garlic, minced 1/4 cup **carrots**, finely chopped 1/4 cup **celery**, chopped
Liquid	6 cups broth[g]	8 cups broth[g]	7 cups broth[g]	1 1/2 T. **lemon** juice 5 cups broth[g]	4 cups broth[g] plus 2 cups water
Legumes		1 cup red lentils, uncooked		2 1/2 cups cooked garbanzo beans	
Seasonings	1 T. oregano 1/2 T. basil 1/4 tsp. pepper salt to taste	2 tsp. turmeric 2 tsp. curry 1 T. plus 1 tsp. fresh **ginger**, minced 1/4 tsp. pepper salt to taste	4 T. **parsley**, chopped 3 T. **Parmesan cheese** 1/2 tsp. pepper salt to taste 2 cups **bread**, cut into small pieces and toasted[h]	1 T. tahini 3 T. fresh **ginger**, minced 1 tsp. cumin 1/4 tsp. pepper salt to taste 2 T. **parsley**, chopped (optional garnish)	1/8 tsp. cayenne pepper 1/4 tsp. sage 1/4 tsp. cumin 1/4 tsp. pepper salt to taste
Puree[h]	none	all	part	all	all

[h] See hints on the previous page.

[g] See guide on page 36.

Mexican Wrap

- For a fast, healthy lunch, fill a pita with fresh vegetables and beans from the salad bar.

- Blend $1/2$ cup tofu or yogurt with 2 T. peanut butter or tahini (ground sesame seeds) and 2 tsp. lemon juice for a quick sandwich spread. Add vegetables and/or a lean protein such as chicken or turkey.

Sandwiches

Healthy
HINTS

To increase consumption of fruits and vegetables and decrease fat in your meal plan, try having more vegetarian rather than meat sandwiches or add vegetables to sandwiches.

- Change the proportions of sandwich fillers—increase vegetables and decrease the amount of high-fat meats and cheese.

- Add chopped tomatoes, cucumber, celery, or green pepper to tuna salad and chopped apples or apricots to chicken salad.

- Add grilled vegetables (peppers, onions, eggplant, etc.) or roasted red peppers or artichoke hearts from a jar.

- Add sliced tomatoes or red onions; shredded carrots, cabbage or zucchini; or spinach, lettuce or other greens.

A growing variety of meatless soy-based luncheon meats offers the flavors of ham, turkey, sausage, bolognas, and beef with less saturated fat.

Whole grains have more fiber and other health-promoting nutrients than more processed grains. Check the food label to be sure that whole grains are listed as the first ingredient.

Tasty
HINTS

- Condiments such as citrus mustard, salsa, chutney, or a small amount of a gourmet salad dressing can spice up a vegetable-filled sandwich.

- Add variety to sandwiches with different breads including bagels, pitas, tortillas, spring rolls, focaccia, or Armenian lavash (thin, soft, cracker-bread).

- Add zip to low-fat mayonnaise by adding a dash of horseradish or hot pepper sauce, mustard, hoisin sauce, curry powder, or lemon or lime juice.

- Drier breads like French bread are a good choice for moist sandwich fillings, while a more moist bread works well with drier fillings.

- Instead of peanut butter and jelly, try peanut butter and banana slices or peanut butter mixed with grated carrot.

Cooking Directions for the Basic Recipe

Cook chicken or use leftover chicken for the Island and Mexican (optional) versions.

❶ Prepare spread (if needed).

❷ Prepare protein and vegetables. For the Island Chicken and Thai Tuna versions, mix the protein, vegetables, and seasonings together.

❸ Prepare the sandwiches:
- For the Island and Thai versions, use ¼ of the mixture for each sandwich.
- For the Italian, Mexican and Middle Eastern versions, layer or stuff ¼ of each of the ingredients on the bread.

❹ Add the topping and other slice of bread. Roll the tortillas (1 inch at top and bottom, then roll from the sides) for the Mexican and Middle Eastern wraps. Microwave Mexican tortilla to heat, if desired.

Sandwiches
Five International Variations
4 Servings

Ingredients	ISLAND CHICKEN	ITALIAN VEGGIE	MEXICAN WRAP	MIDDLE EASTERN VEGGIE	THAI TUNA
Bread	4 bagels	8 slices Italian bread or baguette	4 whole-wheat flour tortillas	4 whole-wheat pita breads or whole-wheat tortillas	8 slices whole-grain bread
Spread		Puree tomato pesto in blender: 1 cup chopped sun-dried tomatoes with liquid* 2 tsp. olive oil ½ tsp. Italian herb seasoning	1 cup fat-free refried beans	¾ cup hummus (store-bought or see recipe below)	
Protein	2 cups cooked chicken, diced (mixed together with vegetables and seasonings)	4 oz. low-fat mozzarella cheese (4 slices or 8 T. shredded)	1 cup cooked chicken, cut into strips or 4 T. cheddar cheese,ᵍ shredded		1 can (12 oz.) tuna (mixed together with vegetables and seasonings)
Vegetables	1 carrot, grated ¼ cup onion, minced	1 cup arugula or spinach leaves ½ red onion, thinly sliced 2 tomatoes, sliced	½ cup red onion, chopped and/or ½ cup green bell peppers, chopped	1 cup grated carrots 2 tomatoes, chopped 2 cups red cabbage, chopped	¼ cup scallions, chopped
Seasoning	1 tsp. curry powder 2 T. lime juice ½ T. honey 2 T. low-fat mayonnaise or plain yogurt		1 cup salsa (or mix together ½ cup salsa and ½ cup low-fat sour cream)		3 T. lime juice 1½ T. lite soy sauceᵍ 1½ T. fresh ginger, minced 1½ tsp. sesame oil
Topping		Fresh basil leaves, chopped	Fresh cilantro leaves		Bean sprouts 1 cup mixed salad greens

* Soaked in 1½ cups boiling water for 5 minutes.　　ᵍ See guide on page 36.

Hummus: Puree in blender or food processor 2 cans (15 oz.) drained chickpeas, ¼ cup lemon juice, 2 garlic cloves, ¼ tsp. ground cumin, and 3 T. tahini (ground sesame seeds). Process until smooth. Refrigerate unused portion.

11

Healthy Grains

- Choose whole grains such as brown rice, whole-wheat couscous, and whole grain breads whenever possible. These are richer in nutrients and fiber than their more processed counterparts. Although they take longer to cook, the added nutrients, texture, and flavor make them worth the additional preparation time. Quick-cooking brown rice is available.

- Quinoa (KEEN-wa) is technically not a grain but cooks like one. It is a complete protein, which is unusual for a plant food. It is almost gluten-free, making it a good alternative for people with allergies to wheat. Its nutty flavor is highlighted in the Southwestern recipe by the addition of pecans and walnuts.

- Most of the fat in nuts is not saturated. In fact, they're a good source of beneficial fats. Nuts also contain fiber, protein, vitamins and minerals. You can include them in moderate amounts in a healthy diet. Toasting nuts gives them a rich flavor so you can use a smaller amount.

Photo courtesy of the Wheat Foods Council

Helpful

H I N T S

- Cooking times:
  White rice: 20 minutes; *Brown rice:* 45 minutes; *Quinoa*: 15–20 minutes; *Couscous*: add the liquid, stir, and remove from heat; *Whole-wheat couscous:* simmer 5 minutes, let sit 10 minutes.

- Cook extra rice and use it to make another quick meal. The next day, you can reheat the rice, add more vegetables, fish, chicken, or tofu and make a stir-fry!

Tasty

H I N T S

- *To toast the nuts*: Spread the nuts in a single layer on a baking sheet and toast in a 350° oven for 3–5 minutes, or stir in a dry saucepan over low heat for 2–3 minutes. Watch them carefully so that they will be lightly toasted but not burned.

- Try some of the aromatic rices for variety—basmati, texmati, and jasmine. Cook them as you would regular rice.

- Wild rice blends offer another flavor option. Wild rice is actually the seed of a grass and has a strong flavor and chewy texture that goes well with brown rice or barley. These blends usually require about 45 minutes of cooking.

Cooking Directions for the Basic Recipe

❶ Heat the oil in a large saucepan.

❷ Add the vegetables and cook for 2–3 minutes over medium heat.

❸ Add the seasonings and grain and cook for another 2 minutes.

❹ Add the liquid and bring to a boil. Reduce heat and simmer, covered, until the grain is cooked. See previous tips page for cooking times.

❺ Add the toppings and blend all together (let the black beans heat through) before serving.

Five International Variations
Grains
6 to 8 Servings

Ingredients	ASIAN RICE	ITALIAN RICE	MEXICAN RICE	MOROCCAN COUSCOUS	SOUTHWESTERN QUINOA
Oil*	1 T. canola or olive oil	1 T. olive oil	1 T. olive oil	1 T. olive oil	1 T. canola or olive oil
Vegetables	1 cup **onions**, chopped ½ cup **carrots**, grated	¾ cup **onion**, chopped ¼ cup sun-dried tomatoes** (rehydrated and finely chopped)	1½ cups **onion**, chopped	¾ cup red **onion**, chopped	1 cup **onion**, minced
Seasonings	1 T. fresh **ginger**, minced ¼ tsp. pepper salt to taste	2 tsp. garlic, minced 1 T. basil ¼ tsp. pepper salt to taste	1½ T. garlic, minced ¾ tsp. cumin ¼ tsp. pepper salt to taste	1½ tsp. fresh garlic, minced ½ tsp. cinnamon 1½ T. fresh **marjoram**, chopped 2 T. raisins ¼ tsp. pepper salt to taste	1 T. garlic, minced 1½ tsp. ground coriander ½ tsp. pepper salt to taste
Grain	1¼ cups rice[h]	1¼ cups rice[h]	1¼ cups rice[h]	1¼ cups couscous[h]	1½ cups quinoa[†]
Liquid	2½ cups broth[g] 1½ tsp. sesame oil 1½ tsp. lite soy sauce	2 cups water Juice of 1 **orange** (about ½ cup)	2½ cups broth[g] 1 cup cooked black beans	¾ cup tomato juice ¾ cup water	2½ cups broth[g]
Topping	2 T. **scallions**, chopped (optional garnish)	2 T. pine nuts, toasted[h]	3 T. fresh **cilantro**, chopped	2 T. slivered almonds, toasted[h]	2 T. walnut pieces, toasted[h] 2 T. pecans, toasted[h]

*Broth or other liquid can be substituted for the oil.

**Soaked in boiling water for 5 minutes and drained.

[g] See guide on page 36.

[h] See hints on the previous page.

[†] Rinse and drain the quinoa first to remove a bitter residue that sometimes remains on the seeds.

Veggies

Italian Zucchini

Helpful HINTS

- Nothing beats the flavor of fresh vegetables. Other convenient, timesaving options include frozen, canned, pre-cut packaged, and salad bar vegetables.

- You can turn the Mexican Peppers and Onions into fajitas. On a large tortilla, spoon some of the cooked vegetables; fresh chopped tomatoes; shredded lettuce; cheese or cooked, shredded chicken; and salsa.

- You can also steam or microwave the vegetables first. Meanwhile, combine the liquid (omit the water from the carrot and broccoli recipes) and seasonings. Pour the seasoning mixture over the vegetables.

Tasty HINTS

- If vegetables are not one of your favorite foods, keep trying different ones. With the wide variety of colors, flavors and textures to choose from, you're sure to find some you like. Try them raw or cooked.

- Use vegetables that are in season whenever possible.

- *To steam vegetables:* Cut vegetables into chunks and place in a metal steamer. Place the steamer into a pot that has about an inch of boiling water in it. Add vegetables, cover the pot, and adjust the heat to keep the water simmering. Cook until the vegetables are cooked to desired tenderness, adding additional water if necessary.

Healthy HINTS

- Eat a wide variety of deeper-colored vegetables and fruit. In general, these have the most nutrients. Beneficial plant substances called phytochemicals are what give plants their rich color and flavor.

- When shopping for vegetables, buy 3 different colors for variety in flavor and nutrients.

- Eat a minimum of five servings of fruits and vegetables each day for optimal health. Most people underestimate the amount to buy. For example, if there are 4 people in your family and you shop for 5 days of groceries, you'll need to buy 100 servings! A serving is $1/2$ cup of cooked vegetables, 1 cup leafy vegetables, or 1 medium fruit.

Cooking Directions for the Basic Recipe

❶ Add all the liquid and seasonings to a large saucepan, stir together, and heat.

❷ Add the vegetables and cook on medium heat until the vegetables are cooked to desired tenderness. (About 5–10 minutes for all except the carrots, which take 15–20 minutes)

If the vegetables begin to stick to the bottom of the pan as you cook them, add a little more water. See previous cooking tips page for more vegetable cooking options.

Five International Variations'
Veggies
4 to 6 Servings

Ingredients	ASIAN CARROTS	FRENCH BROCCOLI	ITALIAN ZUCCHINI	MEXICAN PEPPERS & ONIONS	IRISH GREEN BEANS ......
Liquid	2 tsp. canola oil or olive oil 1 tsp. sesame oil ¼ cup water*	1 T. fresh **lemon** juice ½ cup water	2 tsp. olive oil 1 tsp. red wine vinegar	1 T. olive oil juice of 1 **lime**	½ cup malt vinegar**
Seasonings	2 tsp. fresh **ginger**, minced 1 T. sesame seeds, toasted 2 tsp. fresh **cilantro**, chopped, optional ⅛ tsp. pepper salt to taste	2 T. almonds, crushed 3 T. fresh **parsley**, finely chopped 1½ tsp. lemon zest ¼ tsp. pepper salt to taste	½ T. garlic, minced 1 tsp. oregano 1 tsp. basil salt and pepper to taste	½ tsp. chili powder 2–3 tsp. cumin salt to taste	1½–2 T. brown sugar salt and pepper to taste
Vegetables	8 large **carrots**, chopped ½ cup chopped **scallions**	4½ cups **broccoli**	2 **green zucchini**[†] 2 **yellow zucchini squash**[†] 1 **carrot**[†] [†]cut all into 2-inch chunks and then into thin ¼-inch strips	2 **red peppers**, thinly sliced 2 **green peppers**, thinly sliced 1 **onion**, thinly sliced	5 cups green beans, trimmed and cut into 2" lengths (or substitute 1 small head of cabbage)

* 2 T. of orange juice can be substituted for 2 T. of water.
** For a sweeter flavor, you can use balsamic vinegar.

Chicken, Fish, & Soy

Tasty
HINTS

- Dry marinades or rubs (as in the Cajun chicken recipe) are an easy way to add flavor. The mixture of herbs and spices can be made in large quantities and stored in jars for later use.

Asian Tofu and Rice

Helpful
HINTS

- Pat the tofu dry with paper towels before marinating to allow more of the marinade to be absorbed.

- For an attractive presentation, slice the cooked chicken into thin slices and fan it on the plate. Cut the tofu in half diagonally and then in half a second time, again diagonally. Serve over rice.

- Instead of baking or grilling, cut the marinated food into pieces and sauté in a pan with assorted, chopped vegetables. Serve over rice or noodles.

- *Bake*: Chicken—350°, approximately 20–30 minutes, until the chicken is firm and fully cooked. Fish—450°, about 10 minutes per inch of thickness at thickest part, or until fish is just opaque and flakes when tested with a fork. Soy—350°, about 15 minutes. Optional: broil the chicken, fish, or soy for a minute or two at the end of baking to brown.

- *Grill*: About 3–10 minutes on each side. Use any extra marinade to baste the food as it cooks on the grill. If grilling the Cajun chicken, brush lightly with olive oil before cooking.

Healthy
HINTS

- Instead of having meat or chicken at the center of the plate, use it more as a condiment with serving sizes of about 3 ounces (3 ounces is the size of a deck of cards). Serve with larger amounts of grains and vegetables.

- Fish and poultry are good choices since they are low in saturated fat. Fish, particularly fattier fish such as salmon and tuna, contain a beneficial type of unsaturated fat called omega 3 fatty acids.

- Most of the fat in tofu and other soy products is unsaturated. The soybean is a complete protein since it contains all the essential amino acids.

- Diversify your protein intake by including more plant sources—beans, grains, nuts, and seeds. These foods are also a good source of fiber and other nutrients.

Cooking Directions for the Basic Recipe

❶ Mix marinade together in a bowl.

❷ Place the fish, chicken, or tofu in a baking dish and cover it with the marinade. Turn to coat. For more flavor, let it marinate for at least 20 minutes, refrigerated, turning it from time to time.

❸ Spray a baking dish with cooking oil or brush lightly with oil. Bake or grill until cooked. Test for doneness. See baking hints on the previous page.

❹ Cut into individual serving sizes[h] and serve with vegetables and/or salad and a grain.

Five International Variations
Chicken, Fish, & Soy

4 to 5 Servings

Ingredients	ASIAN TOFU	CAJUN CHICKEN	CUBAN FISH	FRENCH SALMON	MEDITERRANEAN CHICKEN
	......	......	......	......	......
Marinade	2 T. lite soy sauce[g] 1–2 T. sesame oil 1 tsp. fresh garlic, minced 2 tsp. brown sugar or orange juice 1 tsp. fresh **ginger**, minced 1/8 tsp. cayenne pepper	1 T. paprika 1 tsp. thyme 1 tsp. oregano 1/2 tsp. garlic powder 1/8 tsp. cayenne pepper 1/2 tsp. salt	1/4 cup fresh **lime** juice (juice of 2 limes) 1/2 T. olive oil 1/2 T. fresh garlic, minced 2 T. fresh oregano, chopped or 2 tsp. dried 1/8 tsp. pepper pinch salt pinch cumin	3 T. white wine 2 tsp. dill 1 tsp. garlic powder or fresh minced 1/8 tsp. pepper 1 **lemon**, thinly sliced (arrange lemon slices over fish before cooking and use as garnish)	2 T. balsamic vinegar 2 tsp. Dijon mustard 1/2 T. olive oil 1 T. fresh garlic, minced 1/2 tsp. oregano 1/4 tsp. pepper
Chicken, Fish or Soy	1 lb. firm or extra firm **tofu**[h], cut in half horizontally, pressed to remove extra water	1 lb. boneless, skinless **chicken**	1 lb. **halibut** or any firm white fish	1 lb. **salmon**	1 lb. skinless, boneless **chicken**

[g] See guide on page 36.

[h] See hints on the previous page.

Pizza

Quick Pizza Crust

2 cups all-purpose flour

1 pkg. Rapid-Rise yeast

1/2 tsp. sugar

3/4 tsp. salt

3/4 cups warm water

1 tsp. olive oil

In food processor, combine the flour, yeast, sugar and salt. Mix the warm water (125 degrees) and oil and gradually add to the food processor while the motor is running.

Process until the dough forms a ball, adding up to 2 T. cold water, if necessary. Process an additional minute to knead. Turn out onto a lightly floured surface. Cover with plastic wrap and let rest for 10 minutes. Shape into one large crust or 4–6 individual crusts.

Tasty
H I N T S

- For variations of the Quick Pizza Crust recipe, try adding seasonings such as oregano, basil, or thyme. You can also substitute 1 cup whole-wheat flour, cornmeal, or other flour.

Helpful
H I N T S

- To make these pizzas, you can either make your own crust using the recipe provided or you can purchase a prepared crust. Other options for quick crusts are frozen bread doughs, tortillas, French bread, pita bread, or Italian flat breads.

- For a crispy crust, bake the crust on a pizza stone or tile or on an inverted cookie sheet dusted with cornmeal.

- Make extra crusts to have ready for fast pizza dinners during the week. (Store the individual doughs in plastic wrap in the refrigerator for up to 2 days or in the freezer for up to 2 months. Bring to room temperature before using.)

- Vegetables such as broccoli and eggplant can be cooked before adding them to the pizza, if desired.

- For a thinner spread on the Mexican pizza, mix some of the salsa with the refried beans.

Mediterranean Pizza

Cooking Directions for the Basic Recipe

❶ Prepare crust. Preheat oven to 400 degrees.

❷ Prepare spread.

❸ Spray a large cookie sheet with a vegetable oil spray and place the crust(s) on the sheet.

❹ Cover crust with the spread.

❺ Add toppings and cheese, if used.

❻ Bake at 400 degrees for approximately 12–15 minutes or until bubbly.

Five International Variations
Pizza
4 to 6 Servings

Ingredients	ASIAN	GREEK	ITALIAN	MEDITERRANEAN	MEXICAN
Crust	1 ready-to-use **crust**[h]	6 **pita breads** or 1 ready-to-use **crust**[h]	1 ready-to-use **crust**[h] or 1 large Italian **flatbread**	1 ready-to-use **crust**[h]	6 flour **tortillas** or 1 ready-to-use **crust**[h]
Spread	Mix the following together and then cook 2–3 minutes over medium heat: 1/4 cup rice vinegar 1/4 cup pineapple juice (from tidbits) 2 T. lite soy sauce 1 T. cornstarch 1 tsp. garlic, minced 1 tsp. **fresh ginger,** minced 1/4 tsp. pepper	Puree in blender: 1/2 cup raisins 2 T. **onion,** chopped 1/3 cup water	Cook the following over medium heat for 5 minutes: 16 oz. canned tomato sauce 1 **carrot,** grated 3 T. **fresh basil,** chopped 1/2 tsp. oregano 1/4 tsp. pepper	Puree in blender: 1 T. olive oil 1/3 cup water 3 T. tomato paste 1 1/2 cups fresh **basil** 3 cloves garlic 1/4 cup **Romano** or **Parmesan** cheese 1 T. pine nuts or walnuts, salt	1 cup fat-free refried beans
Toppings	1 cup each, chopped: **red pepper, broccoli** 1 cup water chestnuts, sliced 1/2 cup pineapple tidbits 1/2 cup **bean sprouts**	Chop finely in large bowl: 2 cups **fresh spinach** (tightly packed) 1 cup **scallions** Add 1 T. pine nuts 1 T. olive oil 1/4 cup **lemon juice** 1/8 tsp. allspice 1/8 tsp. pepper dash salt	1 cup artichoke hearts, quartered 1/2 cup thinly sliced sun-dried tomatoes* 2 T. chopped black olives	1 cup each, thinly sliced: **mushrooms** or **egg-plant** **plum tomatoes** **red onion**	1/2 cup each, diced: **green chilies, onion** 1 cup plum **tomatoes,** sliced 1 cup **bell pepper,** diced 1 cup salsa
Cheese	1/2 cup firm **tofu,** crumbled	1/2 cup crumbled **feta cheese,** optional	1/2 cup **mozzarella cheese,** grated		1/2 cup **cheddar cheese,** grated

*Soaked in boiling water for 5 minutes and drained.

[h] See hints on the previous page.

Stews

Healthy
HINTS

- Stews are an easy and delicious way to add fiber-rich foods to your diet. Fiber is found only in food from plant sources. High-fiber foods produce a full feeling and are usually low in fat. The soluble fiber in foods such as beans, fruits, and vegetables helps regulate blood sugar levels and lowers blood cholesterol.

- Aim for at least 25 grams of fiber each day. Beans and lentils have approximately 8 grams of fiber per 3/4 cup; vegetables, fruits, and whole grains have about 2 grams per 1/2 cup; and nuts and seeds have about 3 grams per ounce.

- Canned tomatoes are a good source of lycopene, a health-promoting phytochemical.

Helpful
HINTS

For convenience in adding vegetables:

- Chop a large quantity of frequently used vegetables such as onions and green peppers and freeze in a zippered plastic bag or airtight container for future meals.

- Add frozen vegetables to the stew for the last 5 minutes of cooking.

- Add pre-chopped vegetables from the supermarket salad bars or leftover vegetables from your fridge.

To freeze soups or stews: Pour into an airtight container, leaving enough room for expansion (an inch or two at the top). To reheat, thaw completely in the refrigerator, then place contents in a saucepan over low heat, adding some liquid if necessary.

Tasty
HINTS

- Make extra amounts of stews. Many are even better the next day as the flavors blend.

- When cooking with less fat, increase the amount of seasoning to boost flavor.

- To keep the vegetables in the stew from becoming mushy, cut them into large, uniform chunks. Add slower-cooking, denser vegetables such as carrots and potatoes first before adding juicier ones such as zucchini or tomatoes.

- Many ingredients can be used to thicken a stew, including soft, creamy vegetables (potatoes, yams, and squash); beans or split peas; tahini or peanut butter; and grains such as cornmeal, rice, or bulghur.

Moroccan Stew

Cooking Directions for the Basic Recipe

(If serving the stew over a longer-cooking grain such as brown rice, time the cooking process so the grain will be cooked when the stew is cooked, or reheat a previously cooked grain.)

❶ Prepare all vegetables and seasonings.

❷ Heat the oil in large pot over medium heat.

❸ Cook onions and seasonings for 3–5 minutes or until onions are soft.

❹ Add the remaining vegetables.

❺ Add the liquid, the thickener, and the ad lib. Cover and simmer for 25 minutes or until all ingredients are cooked and at desired tenderness.
(The fish in the Creole version can be added in the last 10 minutes.)

❻ Serve as is or over brown rice, couscous, or with whole-grain bread.

Five International Variations
Stews
4 to 5 Servings

Ingredients	SOUTHWESTERN CORN	MEXICAN BEAN	MOROCCAN VEGETABLE	CREOLE FISH	AFRICAN SWEET POTATO
Vegetables	1 small **onion**, finely chopped 1 cup **green beans**, cut into 1" pieces, optional 1 can (14.5 oz.) tomatoes 2 cups **corn** kernels, fresh or frozen	1 **onion**, chopped 2 **carrots**, finely chopped 1 cup **celery**, diced 1 cup **green pepper**, chopped 1 can (28 oz.) diced tomatoes	1 **onion**, diced 4 **carrots**, chopped 1 **red bell pepper**, chopped 2 **zucchini**, chopped 1 can (14.5 oz.) whole tomatoes	1 **onion**, chopped 1 cup **celery**, chopped 2 **green bell peppers**, chopped 2 cups **tomatoes**, chopped (fresh or canned)	1 **onion**, chopped 1 can (18 oz.) yams,** drained and chopped 4 cups **cabbage**, chopped 1 can (14.5 oz.) diced tomatoes, undrained
Seasoning	1–2 cloves garlic, minced	2 cloves garlic, minced 1½ T. chili powder ½ tsp. ground cumin 1 T. minced **jalapeno pepper**	1 T. fresh **ginger**, minced 2 tsp. cinnamon ¾ tsp. turmeric	2 cloves garlic, minced 2 tsp. dried basil ½ tsp. dried thyme ¼ tsp. ground allspice ⅛ tsp. cayenne pepper	3 cloves garlic, minced 2 T. fresh **ginger**, minced 1½ T. ground coriander ⅛ tsp. cayenne pepper
Oil*	1 T. olive oil	1 T. olive oil	1 T. olive oil	1 T. olive oil	1 T. olive oil
Liquid	5 cups vegetable or chicken broth[g] 1 T. **lime juice**	2 cups vegetable or chicken broth[g]	1 cup water	4 cups vegetable broth[g] or water	2½ cups water 1 can (6 oz.) tomato paste
Thickener	½ cup cornmeal	1 can (6 oz.) tomato paste		½ cup rice, uncooked	3–4 T. peanut butter
Ad Lib[a]	12 oz. textured **soy product**[h] or 12 oz. diced **chicken**	1 can (15 oz.) kidney or pinto beans, drained or 12 oz. ground **turkey**	1½ cups cooked garbanzo or kidney beans	12 oz. firm **fish** (such as cod, snapper, or grouper). The fish will break up as it cooks.	

*If vegetables become dry, add a little water.

[a] Use the suggested ingredient or substitute your own special ingredient such as chicken, turkey, fish, lean meat, soy products[h], or beans.

[g] See guide on page 36.

[h] See soy hints on page 30.

**2 sweet potatoes or yams, peeled and cut into 1/2" pieces, can be substituted. Boil until just tender before adding to the stew or add them uncooked and increase the cooking time of stew by about 15 minutes.

Spanish Pasta

Pasta

Tasty HINTS

- For variety and added nutrients, try whole grain pastas, flavored pastas, and pastas made from other flours such as corn, rice, quinoa, and amaranth.

- Asian noodles made from buckwheat, rice, wheat, or beans offer additional flavor and texture options. Udon noodles are made from whole wheat flour.

Healthy HINTS

- Grains and grain products such as pasta should be the major source of calories in our diet. Six to eleven servings each day is recommended with at least three being whole grains. A serving is equivalent to one slice of bread or $1/2$ cup of cereal, pasta, rice or other grain. Most grains have less than 200 calories per cooked cup, no cholesterol, only a trace of fat, and contain many nutrients.

- Most fresh pastas are made with eggs and contain 55 mg of cholesterol and slightly more fat per cooked cup than dried varieties.

How to Make Sauces Lower in Fat

Any of these methods can be used to make flavorful sauces:

Substitute evaporated skim milk for cream.

Add $1/3$ cup nonfat dry milk to one cup of skim milk. Use in place of cream or whole milk.

For creamy chicken, fish, or beef flavored sauces, add $1/3$ cup nonfat dry milk to broth and add a little wine or sherry.

Cornstarch or flour can be used as thickeners instead of higher fat ingredients. Flour can be used to thicken gravies and white or brown sauces, while cornstarch works well for translucent sauces. To thicken $1^1/2$–2 cups of liquid, mix 1 T. cornstarch or 2–4 T. flour with a small amount of cold liquid and add to the sauce. When cornstarch is used, add the mixture to the sauce during the last 2 minutes of cooking. When using flour, allow the sauce to simmer at least 3 minutes after adding the flour mixture.

Extra seasonings can be used to add flavor to low-fat sauces.

Cooking Directions for the Basic Recipe

❶ Cook pasta according to package directions.

❷ Prepare all vegetables and seasonings.

❸ Place cooking liquid in saucepan over medium-high heat.

❹ Add vegetables and seasonings and cook for 3–7 minutes.

❺ Add the ad lib and cook for 3–5 minutes or until all food is heated and cooked to desired tenderness.

❻ Pour vegetable mixture over the hot pasta.

Five International Variations
Pasta
4 to 6 Servings

Ingredients	ASIAN	FRENCH	ITALIAN	MEXICAN	SPANISH
Pasta	12 oz. udon noodles (or linguine)[g]	10 oz. pasta shells[g]	10 oz. ziti[g]	10 oz. bow tie pasta[g]	10 oz. penne pasta[g]
Vegetables	1 cup each: **carrots**, thinly sliced **scallions**, chopped **snow peas**, **bean sprouts**, 2 cups **mushrooms**, sliced	1 cup **onions**, diced 2 cups each: **zucchini**, **plum tomatoes**, **mushrooms**, chopped	3 cups **tomatoes**, chopped 2 cups **zucchini**, sliced 1 cup **onions**, finely chopped	3 cups **tomatoes**, diced 1 cup **onion**, finely diced 7 oz. can green chilies	2 cups **red pepper** 1 cup **yellow or green pepper** (all peppers cut in thin strips) 1 cup **onion**, thinly sliced 1 cup of artichoke hearts, quartered
Seasonings	2 tsp. garlic, minced 1 T. **fresh ginger**, grated 1/4 tsp. red pepper flakes	1 T. garlic, minced 2 T. **fresh basil**, chopped 1/4 cup **fresh parsley**, chopped 1/4 tsp. pepper salt	2 tsp. garlic, minced 2-3 **anchovies**, optional 1 tsp. oregano 1/2 tsp. sage 1/2 tsp. marjoram	1 T. garlic, chopped 1/4 tsp. cumin salt	2 tsp. garlic, minced 1 tsp. thyme 1/4 cup **fresh parsley**, chopped 1/4 tsp. pepper salt
Cooking Liquid	1 T. sesame oil 3 T. lite soy sauce 1/3 cup rice vinegar 1/3 cup white wine or broth	1/2 cup **clam juice** 1/2 cup white wine	3/4 cup broth 1/2 cup white wine 1 T. olive oil 2 T. tomato paste	1/2 cup broth and 1 cup salsa	1 T. olive oil 3/4 cup broth 2 T. **lemon juice**
Ad Lib[a]	1 cup cooked **chicken**, cut into strips or 2 T. peanuts	8 oz. **bay scallops** or any firm **white fish** cut into 1 inch chunks (such as cod, snapper, or grouper); 1 cup evaporated fat-free milk mixed with 3 T. flour 1/4 cup **grated parmesan cheese**, optional	1 cup cooked cannellini beans[g]	1 1/2 cups cooked, diced **chicken** or cooked pinto beans[g]	6 oz. tuna or 1/3 cup **parmesan cheese**

[g] See guide on page 36.

[a] Use one of the suggested ingredients or substitute your own special ingredient.

Helpful
H I N T S

- Canned tomatoes are a convenient and flavorful alternative to fresh tomatoes in many recipes. Canned tomatoes are simply fresh, red, ripe tomatoes, while jarred pasta sauces often have added salt, sugar, and other ingredients that add calories.

- If you don't use the entire can of tomato products, store the extra in a glass container in the refrigerator.

- Two ounces of dry pasta makes about 1 cup cooked.

- Heat leftover vegetables or chicken, add a prepared pasta sauce, and toss with cooked pasta for a quick meal.

- For a quick marinara sauce, sauté garlic and onion in olive oil; add canned tomatoes, seasonings, and/or fresh basil; and cook for 10–15 minutes. Add mushrooms, artichokes, or capers if desired.

Tasty
H I N T S

- Grind nuts with fresh herbs to create a pesto. The usual pesto is made with basil, pine nuts, and olive oil. For variety, try almonds, cashews, or walnuts and other herbs. For example, a pesto made from cashews and cilantro and seasoned with hot red peppers and soy sauce has a Thai twist. For a lower fat version of pesto, substitute vegetable or chicken broth for half or most of the oil.

- To make a cold pasta salad: Add veggies (diced tomatoes, zucchini, peppers, for example) to cooked pasta. Toss with a little olive oil and Parmesan cheese or a low-fat bottled or homemade vinaigrette dressing. Have your dressing ready and toss with hot noodles to let the dressing sink in better. Then chill before serving.

Healthy
H I N T S

- Pasta has the same amount of calories as other carbohydrate foods: 4 calories per gram (112 calories per ounce).

- Add lots of nutrient- and fiber-rich vegetables to pasta to make the meal more filling and satisfying without adding too much fat or extra calories.

- Grain-based foods, including pasta, are now fortified with folic acid, which plays an important part in the body's central nervous system.

- To keep pasta from sticking together, cook it in a large amount of water, at least a gallon for one pound of pasta. Add to the water gradually to maintain a boil, and stir for the first few minutes.

Cooking Directions for the Basic Recipe

❶ Cook pasta according to package directions.

❷ Prepare all vegetables and seasonings.

❸ Heat the oil and sauté the garlic (and onion for the Southwestern mole) over medium heat (30 seconds for the garlic, 3 minutes for the onion).

❹ Add remaining seasonings and vegetables and cook for 3–7 minutes.

❺ Add the liquid and the "ad lib" and cook for 7–10 minutes or until all food is heated and cooked to desired tenderness. The cheeses in the Greek and Mediterranean versions and the parsley in the Portuguese version can be added as a topping just before serving.

❻ Pour sauce over the hot pasta.

Five International Variations
More Pasta
4 to 6 Servings

Ingredients	JAPANESE	GREEK	MEDITERRANEAN	PORTUGUESE	SOUTHWESTERN CHOCOLATE MOLE
Pasta	10 oz. udon noodles[g] or linguine	12 oz. fettuccine[g]	12 oz penne pasta[g]	10 oz. bow-tie pasta[g] or shells	10 oz. ziti **[g]
Vegetables	2 large **carrots**, grated 2 **scallions**, chopped 2 cups **Napa cabbage**	1 large bunch **spinach**, chopped 1 can (28 oz.) tomatoes, undrained	2 cups **broccoli**, chopped 1 **carrot*** 2 **zucchini**, cut into 2" lengths and then into 1/4" strips 14.5 oz. can tomatoes (or 5 plum tomatoes, chopped)	3/4 cup sun-dried tomatoes, sliced, with liquid* 4 cups **mushrooms**, sliced	1/2 cup **onion**, finely chopped 15 oz. can tomato sauce 1 T. chopped **chili pepper**, optional
Seasoning	1 clove garlic, minced 2 T. fresh **ginger**, minced 1/8 tsp. red pepper flakes	2 large cloves garlic, minced 1/2 tsp. oregano 1/8 tsp. pepper salt, optional	2 cloves garlic, minced 1/4 cup fresh (or 1 T. dried) **basil** 1/8 tsp. red pepper flakes salt, optional	3 cloves garlic, minced 1/8 tsp. cayenne pepper 3/4 T. paprika	1 1/2 tsp. chili powder 1 tsp. ground cumin 1/2 tsp. dried oregano 1 T. unsweetened cocoa powder
Oil	1 T. canola oil	1 T. olive oil	1 T. olive oil	1 T. olive oil	1 T. olive oil
Cooking Liquid	3 T. lite soy sauce[g] 1/2 cup vegetable or chicken broth[g] (or water) 1/3 cup rice wine vinegar 1 tsp. sesame oil	1 T. **lemon juice**		2 cups fish or vegetable broth[g]	If sauce is too thick, add a little water or broth
Ad Lib[a]	2 T. peanut butter	1/3 cup **feta cheese**, crumbled	1/4 cup **Parmesan cheese**, grated	12 oz. firm white **fish** (such as cod, snapper, or orange roughy) cut into bite-sized pieces, or scallops 3 T. fresh **parsley**, chopped (optional garnish)	12 oz. cooked **chicken**, cut into bite-sized pieces 1 T. toasted almonds, optional

[a] Use the suggested ingredient or substitute your own special ingredient such as chicken, turkey, fish, lean meat, beans or soy products (see soy hints on page 30).

[g] See guide on page 36.

*Soaked in 1 cup boiling water for 5 minutes.

**The mole sauce is also delicious over rice or warm tortillas. Garnish with shredded lettuce and tomatoes.

Sauté

Helpful
H I N T S

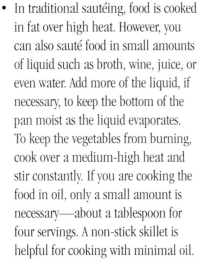

- In traditional sautéing, food is cooked in fat over high heat. However, you can also sauté food in small amounts of liquid such as broth, wine, juice, or even water. Add more of the liquid, if necessary, to keep the bottom of the pan moist as the liquid evaporates. To keep the vegetables from burning, cook over a medium-high heat and stir constantly. If you are cooking the food in oil, only a small amount is necessary—about a tablespoon for four servings. A non-stick skillet is helpful for cooking with minimal oil.

- Use fresh ginger root in these recipes. (Ground ginger is used primarily for baked items.) Fresh ginger can be stored in a plastic bag in the refrigerator for three weeks or in the freezer indefinitely.

Tasty
H I N T S

- For added flavor, marinate the tofu in 2 T. soy sauce, 2 T. rice or cider vinegar, and 1 T. minced fresh ginger for at least 20 minutes.

- To enhance the flavor and aroma of the Indian spices, roast them first. Add the spices to a heavy preheated sauté pan and roast over low heat until they are light brown, shaking the pan or stirring to avoid burning. The spices can also be roasted in a small amount of oil.

- *To toast almonds*: Spread the nuts in a single layer on a baking sheet and toast in a 350°oven for 3–5 minutes or stir in a dry saucepan over low heat for 2–3 minutes. Watch them carefully so that they will be lightly toasted but not burned.

- For variety and added flavor and texture in the rice dishes:

    Try cooking another grain with the rice. For example, add some wheat berries, quinoa, barley, or wild rice.

    Cook the rice in other liquids such as broth, diluted juice, or flavored tea.

    For a richer, nuttier flavor, toast the grains in a dry pan over low heat for 10 minutes before cooking in the liquid.

- Try leftover grains for breakfast. Add juice or milk (low-fat, soy, or rice), raisins or other chopped fruit, and season with cinnamon and vanilla.

Healthy
H I N T S

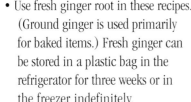

- Whole grains are higher in fiber, vitamin E, and several other vitamins and minerals.

- Brown rice has a chewier texture than white rice and is available in a quick cooking form.

- Basmati rice, commonly used in Indian cooking, has a nutlike fragrance and flavor. Couscous, a "pasta" popular in Northern Africa, is made from semolina wheat. Both are available in whole-grain versions.

Cooking Directions for the Basic Recipe

❶ Begin cooking the grain.

❷ Prepare all vegetables and seasonings.

❸ Heat the sauté liquid in a large skillet. Add vegetables and seasonings. Cook on medium-high heat for 2–3 minutes.

❹ Add the cooking liquid and the ad lib. Cook until all ingredients are at desired tenderness (3–7 minutes).

❺ Serve vegetable mixture over cooked grain.

Five International Variations
Sauté
4 to 6 Servings

Ingredients	ASIAN	INDIAN	INDONESIAN	MEXICAN	MOROCCAN
Grain	1¼ cups rice[g]	1¼ cups basmati rice[g]	1¼ cups rice[g]	1¼ cups rice[g]	1¼ cups couscous[g]
Vegetables	2 cups each: **carrots**, thinly sliced **broccoli**, chopped 3 cups **mushrooms**, sliced	2 cups **carrots**, finely diced 1 cup each, diced: **celery, apples, onions**	1 cup each, chopped: **onion, scallions** 2 cups **green beans**, trimmed and cut in 2" lengths ¼ cup raisins	2 cups each, diced: **onions, bell pepper** 1 cup **tomatoes**, chopped 7-oz. can green chilies, ½ cup black olives, sliced	1 cup each, chopped: **onion, cabbage** 2 cups each, chopped: **tomato, bell pepper**
Seasonings	1 T. fresh **ginger**, grated 2 tsp. garlic, minced ¼ tsp. pepper	1 tsp. ground cardamom[h] 1 tsp. ground coriander ¼ tsp. cinnamon ⅛ tsp. ground cloves ¼ tsp. ground cumin ⅛ tsp. ground pepper (or 1 T. garam masala or curry powder)	1 T. garlic, minced 1 T. curry powder salt	2 tsp. garlic, minced ½ tsp. chili powder ½ cup **fresh cilantro**, chopped	½ tsp. cinnamon ¼ tsp. nutmeg ¼ tsp. pepper dash salt 2 T. raisins
Sauté Liquid	¼ cup broth	1 T. canola oil	Liquid from canned tomatoes	1 T. canola or olive oil	¼ cup white wine
Cooking Liquid	¼ cup orange juice ¼ cup broth 2 T. lite soy sauce 1 T. rice vinegar 2 tsp. sesame oil*	1 cup of broth	28-oz. can tomatoes, chopped	1 cup tomato juice	1 cup broth
Ad Lib[a]	8 oz. **fish** cut into small chunks (firm fish such as orange roughy, grouper, or snapper) or 1 cup firm **tofu**[h] diced	2 T. slivered almonds, toasted[h] 1 cup cooked garbanzo beans[g] or 1 cup cooked **chicken**, optional	2 T. peanut butter	1 cup cooked black beans[g]	1 cup cooked **chicken**, diced

*To thicken the Asian cooking liquid: Mix 1 T. cornstarch with 2 T. cold water and stir in during last 2 minutes of cooking.

[h] See hint on roasting spices on the previous page.

[g] See guide on page 36.

[a] Use one of the suggested ingredients or substitute your own special ingredient.

Stir-Fry

Healthy
H I N T S

- Most deep green leafy vegetables are a good source of iron, calcium, folacin, and beta-carotene. Foods containing vitamin C, such as tomatoes or peppers, enhance the body's absorption of iron from plant foods.

- In the Indian version, coconut milk can be used in place of all or some of the milk. Although coconut milk is high in saturated fat, a small amount goes a long way in adding flavor and texture. Lower-fat versions are also available.

Tasty
H I N T S

- For a variation, add chicken, fish, tofu or beans. For example, Asian—add chicken or tofu; Indian—add garbanzo beans; Mexican—add chicken or beans; Thai—add shrimp.

- Cut the fish or poultry into bite-sized pieces and cook in the oil for a few minutes. Remove from the pan while the vegetables are cooked, and return to the pan with the flavorings.

Helpful
H I N T S

- Cut the greens into 1/2"-wide strips and add to the skillet in batches, adding more as each batch wilts.

- Mirin is a sweet Japanese cooking wine made from rice. Sweet sherry can be substituted.

- Thai ingredients are available in many supermarkets and specialty shops.

Japanese Stir-Fry

❶ Begin cooking the grain.

❷ Prepare all vegetables.

❸ Heat the oil in a skillet or wok. Add the seasonings and nuts and cook, stirring, for 20 seconds to 1 minute.

❹ Add the vegetables and stir-fry over high heat until vegetables are tender-crisp (3–7 minutes).

❺ Stir in flavoring and heat.

❻ Serve vegetables over the cooked grain.

Five International
Stir-Fry
Variations

4 to 6 Servings

Ingredients	INDIAN	ITALIAN	JAPANESE	MEXICAN	THAI
Grain	1 cup basmati rice[g]	12 oz. fettuccine[g]	12 oz. udon or soba noodles[g]	1 cup rice[g]	1 cup jasmine or other rice[g]
Vegetables	1 large bunch **spinach**, chopped 1 cup **onion**, diced 2 cups **tomatoes**, chopped	1 large bunch **chard**, chopped 2 cups **broccoli**, chopped 2 cup **tomatoes**, chopped	1 large **bok choy**, chopped 2 cups **shitake** or any **mushrooms**, sliced 1 cup **red pepper** strips	1 large bunch **kale** or **collards**, chopped 2 cups **cauliflower**, chopped 1 cup salsa	1 small head **cabbage**, chopped 2 cups **celery**, diced 1 cup **carrot**, grated
Oil	1 T. canola oil	1 T. olive oil	1 T. canola oil	1 T. canola oil	1 T. sesame oil
Seasonings	1 T. curry powder salt, optional	1 T. garlic, minced	1 T. fresh **ginger**, grated	1 T. chili powder 2 tsp. **jalapeno pepper**, minced	1 T. fresh **ginger**, minced 1/4 tsp. Thai chili paste
Nuts	2 T. almonds	1 T. pine nuts, optional	2 T. sesame seeds	2 T. walnuts, chopped or pine nuts	2 T. peanuts
Flavoring	1/4 cup low-fat milk	1/3 cup **Parmesan** cheese 1 T. balsamic vinegar	1 tsp. sesame oil 1 T. mirin 1 T. lite soy sauce	1 cup **fresh cilantro**, chopped 1 T. **lime juice**	3 T. Thai fish sauce 2 T. **lime juice**

[g] See guide on page 36.

More **Stir-Fry**

Healthy HINTS

- Vegetable stir-fries are a quick and easy way to include a variety of green leafy vegetables, cruciferous (cabbage family) vegetables, citrus fruits, and red and orange produce—all foods that contain antioxidants and other health-promoting nutrients.

- Soy protein, when consumed as part of a meal plan low in saturated fat and cholesterol, can play a role in reducing the risk of heart disease.

Helpful HINTS

- A wok is ideal for stir-frying, but you can also use a large heavy skillet that allows all of the vegetables to be exposed to the heat.

- Since stir-fry cooking is quick, have all the ingredients and utensils you need prepared and within easy reach of the stove before you begin.

- Cut the stir-fry vegetables into small, even-sized pieces for quick, even cooking. Add the ones that take the longest to cook (onions, carrots, and broccoli) first. Stir constantly over high heat with a large, flat spatula.

- For a stir-fry shortcut, consider frozen vegetables or pre-cut vegetables from the salad bar.

Tasty HINTS

- A small amount of meat or poultry can go a long way in a stir-fry. Slice or dice it into small pieces so the flavor will be distributed throughout the dish.

- Soy products are a versatile and healthy alternative to meat in many recipes. Firm or extra-firm tofu is best for stir-fries. Baked tofu is already cooked and can be used as you would use sliced chicken or meat. Textured soy protein, which has a chewy texture when rehydrated, can be substituted for ground meat in any recipe such as tacos, sauces, and stews.

Herbs and Spices

Many herbs and spices are being studied for their medicinal and therapeutic benefits. Herbs and spices are also a flavorful solution for low-sodium diets. To turn a standard dish into a totally new one, be adventurous with them!

- Before adding dried herbs to a dish, crumble them in your palm to release their flavor.
- 1 tsp. of dried herbs can be substituted for 1 T. fresh herbs.
- Store herbs and spices in clean, airtight containers in a cool, dark place away from heat, light, and moisture (not over the stove, near a window, or under a bright fluorescent light).
- Herbs such as cilantro, basil, sage, and marjoram are better fresh. Others, such as rosemary, leaf oregano, and bay leaves, are very flavorful even when dried.
- The shelf life of herbs and spices varies, but is about 1-2 years for whole spices and herbs and 6 months-1 year for ground spices and herbs. (Date them when you purchase them.)

Indonesian Stir-Fry

Cooking Directions for the Basic Recipe

(If serving the stir-fry over a longer-cooking grain such as brown rice, time the cooking process so the grain will be cooked when the stir-fry is cooked, or reheat a previously cooked grain.)

❶ Begin cooking the grain.

❷ Prepare all the vegetables and seasonings.

❸ Heat the oil in a skillet or wok. Add the seasonings and cook, stirring, for about 20 seconds.

❹ Add the ad lib and cook for 5 minutes.[b]

❺ Add the vegetables in order given, stirring after each addition. Stir-fry over high heat until vegetables are tender-crisp (3–4 minutes) and ad lib is thoroughly cooked.

❻ Stir in flavorings and heat for 1 minute.

❼ Serve over the cooked grain. Add topping.

Five International Variations
More Stir-Fry
4 to 6 Servings

[b]You can also cook the ad lib thoroughly in this step and remove it from the pan to make more room to cook the vegetables. Add it back to the pan at the last minute of cooking to heat thoroughly.

Ingredients	LATIN	HAWAIIAN	PAN ASIAN	CARIBBEAN	INDONESIAN
Grain	4–6 flour **tortillas** or 1 cup rice[*g]	1 cup rice[*g]	1 cup rice[*g]	1 cup rice[*g]	1 cup basmati or any rice[*g] or noodles[g]
Vegetables/ Fruits	1 medium **onion**, chopped 2 **green peppers**, sliced 2 **red peppers**, sliced	2 cups **carrots**, thinly sliced 2 cups **broccoli**, chopped 1 cup **snow peas** 8-oz. can unsweetened pineapple tidbits (reserve juice)	2 bunches fresh **spinach**, shredded 1 cup **scallions**, chopped 1 large **pear**, sliced 1/4" thick	1½ cups chopped red or yellow **onion** 1 bunch **kale**, cut into thin strips	1 head **Napa cabbage** 1 cup **carrots**, thinly sliced 1 **red bell pepper**, thinly sliced 1 cup **mushrooms**, sliced
Oil**	1 T. olive oil	1 T. canola or peanut oil	1 T. canola oil	1 T. olive or canola oil	1 T. canola oil
Seasoning	1½ tsp. chili powder 1½ tsp. cumin 3/4 tsp. ground coriander 1/8 tsp. cinnamon	2 tsp. fresh **ginger**, minced	1 clove garlic, minced 2 T. fresh **ginger**, minced 1/8 tsp. cinnamon	1/2 tsp. allspice 1/2 tsp. thyme	2 cloves garlic, minced 2 tsp. fresh **ginger**, minced 2 tsp. curry powder
Ad Lib[a]	12 oz. boneless **chicken** breast, thinly sliced	12 oz. firm **fish** (cod, snapper, orange roughy, etc.) cut into bite-sized pieces or tofu[ht]	12 oz. boneless **chicken** breasts, cut into bite-sized pieces	12 oz. **chicken**, thinly sliced or baked tofu[h]	12 oz. diced **chicken** or tofu
Flavoring	1/4 cup **lime juice**[g]	Mix together: reserved pineapple juice 2 T. rice wine vinegar 1 T. soy sauce[g] 1 T. cornstarch	Mix together: 1/4 cup broth[g] or water 2 tsp. lite soy sauce[g] 1 tsp. vinegar 1 tsp. cornstarch	1/4 cup **orange juice** 1/2 cup water or broth 1 T. balsamic vinegar 1 cup **orange segments**	1/4 cup broth[g] 2 T. dry sherry or wine 3 T. lite soy sauce[g]
Topping	1/4 cup chopped **cilantro**, optional Serve tortillas with shredded **lettuce** and chopped **tomatoes**	1/2 cup **bean sprouts**		2 T. almond slivers, toasted	2 T. chopped peanuts

* Preferably brown rice.

**1/2 cup broth, wine, juice or water can be substituted or added to the oil.

[a] Use the suggested ingredient or substitute your own special ingredient such as chicken, turkey, fish, lean meat, soy products,[h] or beans.

[h] See hints on previous page.

[g] See hints on page 36.

[†] For added flavor, marinate tofu in 2 T. soy sauce, 2 T. rice or cider vinegar, and 1 T. minced fresh ginger for at least 20 minutes.

Oven–Baked

Helpful HINTS

- Although this meal takes a little longer to cook, the hands-on preparation time is less than $1/2$ hour.

  Potatoes (white)

  Cook in boiling water for 15 minutes or until tender. Drain and set aside until ready to layer.

  To microwave:

  Cook sliced potatoes for 8 minutes. Although potatoes are not a grain, they are listed under this category for ease in following the recipe and because, like grains, they are rich in carbohydrates.

Healthy HINTS

- Because tofu is almost tasteless and takes on the flavors of the foods it's cooked with, it is very versatile. A good source of protein, calcium, and iron, it has less saturated fat than cheese.

- Sweet potatoes are one of the most nutritious vegetables. They are rich in beta-carotene and contain vitamin C, potassium, and fiber.

Tasty HINTS

- $1^1/2$ cups garbanzo beans (canned or cooked) can be substituted for the lentils.

- For a variation of the Indian version, puree the lentils or garbanzo beans in a blender or food processor.

Cooking Directions for the Basic Recipe

❶ Cook grain (except tortillas) and lentils (if using in the Indian version).

❷ Prepare vegetables and seasonings.

❸ Heat sauté liquid. Add vegetables and cook over medium-high heat for 5 minutes.

❹ Add seasonings and cook an additional 3 minutes. (The Spanish ad lib can be added to the vegetable mixture.)

❺ In a 9 by 13-inch casserole dish coated lightly with vegetable oil, layer half (each): grain, vegetable mixture, and ad lib. Repeat. Drizzle liquid over top, if used.

Five International Variations

Oven-Baked

4 to 6 Servings

Ingredients	FRENCH	SPANISH	ITALIAN	MEDITERRANEAN	MEXICAN
Grain	3 medium baking **potatoes**[h], sliced 1/8" thick	1 cup rice[g]	8 oz. lasagna noodles[g]	1 1/2 cups polenta*[g]	12 corn **tortillas**
Vegetables	1 cup **onion**, chopped 3 cups **zucchini**, chopped 3 cups **tomatoes**, chopped	1 large **onion**, chopped 1 cup **celery**, chopped 1 cup **carrots**, sliced 2 cups **mushrooms**, sliced 2 **green peppers**, chopped	1 cup each, chopped: **scallions** **green peppers** 2 cups each, thinly sliced: **mushrooms, zucchini** 43-oz. canned crushed tomatoes	20 oz. frozen **spinach** (thawed and drained) 3 cups **tomatoes**, chopped 2 cups **mushrooms**, sliced 1/4 cup sliced black olives	1 cup each, diced: **onion, bell pepper, tomatoes** 1 cup **corn** 1 cup salsa
Seasonings	2 tsp. tarragon 1 T. **fresh parsley**, chopped 1/4 tsp. pepper salt	1/4 cup flour 1 1/2 tsp. thyme 1/4 cup fresh **parsley** (or 1 T. dried) 1 1/3 cups fat-free **milk** 1 1/2 cups broth (vegetable or chicken) 2 T. dry sherry or white wine, optional	1 tsp. garlic, minced 2 tsp. basil 2 tsp. oregano 1/4 tsp. pepper dash salt	2 tsp. garlic, minced 3/4 tsp. thyme 3/4 tsp. oregano 1/4 tsp. pepper dash salt	2 tsp. garlic, minced 1 tsp. chili powder
Sauté Liquid	1 T. olive oil or 1/4 cup broth	1 T. olive oil	1 T. olive oil or 1/4 cup broth	1 T. olive oil or 1/4 cup broth	1 T. canola oil or 1/4 cup broth
Ad Lib[a]	3/4 cup **Parmesan cheese**	12 oz. canned tuna or 2 cups cooked **chicken**, diced (add to vegetable mixture)	12 oz. firm **tofu**, mashed and 1/2 cup **Parmesan cheese** or 16 oz. tofu, mashed	5 oz. **feta cheese**, crumbled or **mozzarella cheese**, grated	3/4 cup low-fat **Cheddar** or **Monterey Jack cheese**
Drizzle Liquid	1/3 cup white wine mixed with 2 T. Worcestershire sauce and 2 T. flour		Use some of the vegetable mixture for the top layer		1/3 cup broth

*Cooked in 3 cups of water and 3 cups broth.

[h] See hints on the previous page.

[g] See guide on page 36.

[a] Use one of the suggested ingredients or substitute your own special ingredient.

Desserts

Tasty
HINTS

- Each dessert recipe can be served fresh, cooked, or with other foods. Serve the fruit mixture over yogurt, frozen yogurt or low-fat ice cream, sorbet, cereal, pancakes, waffles and muffins.

- Or wrap the fruit mixture in phyllo dough and bake in a 350° oven for about 10 minutes.

Healthy
HINTS

- Enjoy these fruit dishes as snacks as well as desserts. They're a delicious and easy way to get some of the recommended 2–4 daily servings of fruits, while satisfying a sweet tooth.

- Fruits are a good source of beneficial antioxidants and phytochemicals.

Italian Bella Frutta

Helpful
HINTS

- Make your dessert first, before cooking dinner. This will allow all the flavors to blend and increases the flavor.

- Feel free to adjust the proportions of fruits, as well as the types of fruits used. Take advantage of seasonal fruits and whatever you have on hand. For example, try mango with pineapple or strawberries with bananas.

- In the French Citrus Supreme recipe, strain the raspberry mixture to remove the seeds if you would like a smoother texture.

34

Cooking Directions for the Basic Recipe

❶ Slice or chop the fruit and place into a large bowl.

❷ Mix the liquid and seasonings together in a small bowl. (Depending on the ripeness of fruit, you may need to add a little honey or other sweetener.)

❸ Pour the liquid mixture over the fruit.

Optional: Place fruit mixture in saucepan and heat on medium heat for a few minutes. For a thicker sauce, add 1 tsp. of cornstarch mixed with a little water.

❹ Sprinkle toppings over the fruit mixture.

Five International Variations

Desserts
4 to 6 Servings

Ingredients	HAWAIIAN MEDLEY	ITALIAN BELLA FRUTTA	FRENCH CITRUS SUPREME	AMERICAN APPLE BERRY	NEW ZEALAND DELIGHT ......
Fruits	4 **bananas**, sliced 1 cup pineapple chunks 3 T. raisins	3 **pears**, sliced 1 cup **blueberries**, fresh or frozen	3 **oranges**, peeled and sliced	3 **apples**, chopped 1½ cups **blackberries**, fresh or frozen	2½ cups fresh **strawberries**, sliced 5 **kiwi**, sliced
Liquid	3 T. pineapple juice	2½ T. apple juice concentrate	Puree in a blender: 1 T. **orange juice** 1½ cups fresh or frozen **raspberries** (thawed) 1 tsp. honey	½ cup apple juice concentrate 3 T. vanilla **yogurt**	¼ cup lemon **sorbet** juice of ½ **orange** (about 3 T.)
Seasonings	¼ tsp. allspice	½ tsp. almond flavoring 2 tsp. fresh **basil**, very finely shredded ⅛ tsp. nutmeg		¼ tsp. cinnamon	¼ tsp. dry ginger
Toppings	1 T. unsalted peanuts, crushed	1 T. pine nuts, toasted*	1 T. chopped pecans, toasted*	1 T. walnut pieces, toasted*	1 T. sliced almonds, toasted*

*Toasting nuts—see hints on page 12. Crunchy nut cereal can be used instead of the nuts, if desired.

A Guide to Choosing Ingredients

Reducing Salt and Fat

Beans—In all the recipes calling for cooked beans, canned beans can be used as a convenient alternative to dried beans.

To reduce the amount of sodium in canned beans, drain and rinse or buy low-sodium varieties.

Broth—use vegetable or chicken broth (either homemade, canned, powder, or cubes) in any recipe calling for broth. If you want to reduce sodium, try one of the reduced-sodium or sodium-free products available.

Cheese—you can reduce the amount of fat, saturated fat, and calories in a recipe by using less cheese or by using a reduced-fat version. Tofu and soy cheeses are lower in saturated fat and offer another flavor option. Reduced-fat versions are available.

Soy sauce—use reduced-sodium (lite) versions of soy sauce or tamari for 35–40% less sodium.

Oils—use flavorful oils such as dark (Asian) sesame oil and extra-virgin olive oil. This allows you to use small amounts and still enjoy a rich flavor.

Adding Flavor

When *lemon* or *lime juice* is an ingredient, fresh juice is recommended since it adds a much better flavor than bottled juices.

Some of these recipes include wine as an ingredient. Most of the alcohol evaporates during the cooking process, leaving the flavor of the wine. Broth can be substituted for wine in all of these recipes.

To ensure that all vegetables are cooked to the desired tenderness, you can add those that require more cooking first and the quicker cooking vegetables a couple of minutes later.

Measurements

Herbs and spices—amounts given are for dried herbs and spices unless fresh herbs are specified. When substituting dried herbs for fresh ones, use approximately ¼ the amount.

Salt—specific amounts are not given so that you can vary the amounts to your individual preferences.

The following uncooked ingredients, chopped, equal 1 cup.

Apple	1 medium
Bell pepper	1 medium
Cabbage	⅕ small head
Carrot	2 large
Celery	2 medium stalks
Cucumber	½ medium
Green beans	⅓ lb
Mushrooms	4 oz.
Onion	1 medium
Scallions	5 onions
Tomato	1 medium (or 3 plum)
Zucchini	1 small
Hard cheese, shredded	4 oz.
Parmesan, grated	3 oz.

1 medium clove garlic = 1 tsp., minced
14 oz. canned tomatoes = 2 cups chopped fresh tomatoes

Cooking Grains

The "grain" amount in all of these recipes refers to the uncooked amount.

Rice: In a saucepan, bring to a boil 2 cups of liquid for each cup of rice. Add salt or seasonings, if used. Slowly stir in the rice, cover, and cook over low heat until all the liquid is absorbed:
20 minutes for white rice
45 minutes for brown rice
Fluff with fork. One cup makes 3 cups cooked.

Couscous: Bring 1½ cups water or broth to a boil for each cup of couscous. Add salt or seasonings, if desired. Add couscous, stir, and remove from heat. Cover and let stand 5 minutes. Fluff with fork. One cup makes 2½ cups cooked.

Polenta (coarse ground cornmeal): In a large pot, bring to a boil 4 cups of liquid for each cup of cornmeal. Stir in the cornmeal gradually and stir for about 3 minutes until the mixture thickens. Add salt or seasonings, if used. Reduce heat and simmer, stirring often, for 15–20 minutes or until mixture pulls away from sides of saucepan. One cup makes 3½ cups.

Pasta/Noodles: Gradually add 1 lb. of pasta to 5 qt. of rapidly boiling water. Cook uncovered for approximately 5–12 minutes. (See package directions. Cooking time varies by size and shape.) Two oz. dry makes 1 cup cooked.

Nutritional Analyses

You can use the information below to help you be flexible in planning healthy meals. Because precise nutrition information is not yet available on all foods, the numbers are approximate. Rather than "eating by number," the best way to eat a healthy meal plan is to enjoy the wide variety of foods that are naturally low in fat and high in nutrients and flavor. All of the recipes take this approach. Plant foods are emphasized and animal proteins are used in smaller amounts or are optional.

Optional ingredients are not included in the analysis. If more than one ingredient is suggested, the first one is used in the analysis. Reduced-sodium soy sauce and broth and reduced-fat cheeses and tofu were used for the nutritional analysis. Added salt was not included in the analysis. (One teaspoon has 2300 mg. of sodium).

Salads

Asian
Serving Size: 2 cups

Amount per serving

Calories 140   Calories from fat 50

	% Daily Value*
Total Fat 6g	**9%**
Saturated Fat 0.5g	**4%**
Cholesterol 0mg	**0%**
Sodium 510mg	**21%**
Total Carbohydrate 22g	**7%**
Dietary Fiber 8g	**33%**
Sugars 4g	
Protein 6g	

Vitamin A 190%   Vitamin C 100%

Calcium 15%   Iron 110%

Food Exchanges
2 vegetable, 1 fat, ½ fruit

French
Serving Size: 2 cups

Amount per serving

Calories 120   Calories from fat 60

	% Daily Value*
Total Fat 7g	**11%**
Saturated Fat 0.5g	**3%**
Cholesterol 0mg	**0%**
Sodium 80mg	**3%**
Total Carbohydrate 14g	**5%**
Dietary Fiber 3g	**12%**
Sugars 10g	
Protein 3g	

Vitamin A 60%   Vitamin C 70%

Calcium 6%   Iron 10%

Food Exchanges
1 vegetable, 1 fat, ½ fruit

Greek
Serving Size: 2 cups

Amount per serving

Calories 100   Calories from fat 20

	% Daily Value*
Total Fat 2.5g	**4%**
Saturated Fat 1g	**5%**
Cholesterol 5mg	**1%**
Sodium 200mg	**8%**
Total Carbohydrate 14g	**5%**
Dietary Fiber 8g	**31%**
Sugars 3g	
Protein 8g	

Vitamin A 70%   Vitamin C 60%

Calcium 15%   Iron 10%

Food Exchanges
2 vegetable, ½ fat

Italian
Serving Size: 2 cups

Amount per serving

Calories 100   Calories from fat 30

	% Daily Value*
Total Fat 3.5g	**5%**
Saturated Fat 0g	**0%**
Cholesterol 10mg	**3%**
Sodium 50mg	**2%**
Total Carbohydrate 14g	**5%**
Dietary Fiber 4g	**18%**
Sugars 8g	
Protein 7g	

Vitamin A 60%   Vitamin C 90%

Calcium 6%   Iron 6%

Food Exchanges
2 vegetable, 1 meat

Middle Eastern
Serving Size: 2 cups

Amount per serving

Calories 80   Calories from fat 20

	% Daily Value*
Total Fat 2.5g	**4%**
Saturated Fat 1g	**5%**
Cholesterol 5mg	**2%**
Sodium 135mg	**6%**
Total Carbohydrate 12g	**4%**
Dietary Fiber 3g	**14%**
Sugars 6g	
Protein 5g	

Vitamin A 70%   Vitamin C 100%

Calcium 15%   Iron 15%

Food Exchanges
2 vegetable, ½ fat

Soups

California Vegetable
Serving Size: 1½ cups

Amount per serving

Calories 100   Calories from fat 25

	% Daily Value*
Total Fat 3g	**5%**
Saturated Fat 1.5g	**8%**
Sodium 320mg	**13%**
Total Carbohydrate 16g	**5%**
Dietary Fiber 2g	**8%**
Sugars 5g	
Protein 2g	

Vitamin A 60%   Vitamin C 20%

Calcium 4%   Iron 8%

Food Exchanges
1 vegetable, ½ starch

Indian Curried Lentil
Serving Size: 1½ cups

Amount per serving

Calories 140   Calories from fat 25

	% Daily Value*
Total Fat 2g	**3%**
Saturated Fat 1.5g	**8%**
Sodium 105mg	**4%**
Total Carbohydrate 19g	**6%**
Dietary Fiber 2g	**8%**
Sugars 3g	
Protein 8g	

Vitamin A 10%   Vitamin C 4%

Calcium 6%   Iron 15%

Food Exchanges
1 vegetable, 1 starch

Mediterranean Onion
Serving Size: 1½ cups

Amount per serving

Calories 130   Calories from fat 45

	% Daily Value*
Total Fat 4g	**6%**
Saturated Fat 1g	**5%**
Sodium 190mg	**8%**
Total Carbohydrate 16g	**5%**
Dietary Fiber 2g	**8%**
Sugars 6g	
Protein 6g	

Vitamin A 4%   Vitamin C 20%

Calcium 10%   Iron 8%

Food Exchanges
2 vegetable, ½ starch, ½ fat

Middle Eastern Hummus
Serving Size: 1½ cups

Amount per serving

Calories 130   Calories from fat 45

	% Daily Value*
Total Fat 4g	**6%**
Saturated Fat 1.5g	**8%**
Sodium 320mg	**13%**
Total Carbohydrate 15g	**5%**
Dietary Fiber 3g	**12%**
Sugars 2g	
Protein 6g	

Vitamin A 20%   Vitamin C 15%

Calcium 4%   Iron 15%

Food Exchanges
1 vegetable, 1 starch, ½ fat

Southwestern Yam
Serving Size: 1½ cups

Amount per serving

Calories 180   Calories from fat 25

	% Daily Value*
Total Fat 2g	**3%**
Saturated Fat .5g	**2%**
Sodium 70mg	**3%**
Total Carbohydrate 35g	**12%**
Dietary Fiber 3g	**12%**
Sugars 2g	
Protein 4g	

Vitamin A 20%   Vitamin C 30%

Calcium 4%   Iron 6%

Food Exchanges
2 starch

Sandwiches

Island Chicken
Serving Size: 1 sandwich

Amount per serving

Calories 320 Calories from fat 70

% Daily Value*

Total Fat 8g		**12**%
Saturated Fat 2g		**10**%
Cholesterol 60mg		**20**%
Sodium 360mg		**15**%
Total Carbohydrate 38g		**13**%
Dietary Fiber 6g		**25**%
Sugars 6g		
Protein 27g		

Vitamin A 100%   Vitamin C 8%

Calcium 4%   Iron 15%

Food Exchanges
1 vegetable, 2 starch,
3 lean meat, 1 fat

Italian Veggie
Serving Size: 1 sandwich

Amount per serving

Calories 260 Calories from fat 70

% Daily Value*

Total Fat 7g		**12**%
Saturated Fat 2.5g		**12**%
Cholesterol 10mg		**3**%
Sodium 380mg		**16**%
Total Carbohydrate 39g		**13**%
Dietary Fiber 7g		**27**%
Sugars 8g		
Protein 12g		

Vitamin A 25%   Vitamin C 35%

Calcium 15%   Iron 20%

Food Exchanges
2 vegetable, 2 starch, 1 fat

Mexican Wrap
Serving Size: 1 sandwich

Amount per serving

Calories 210 Calories from fat 35

% Daily Value*

Total Fat 4g		**6**%
Saturated Fat 1g		**5**%
Cholesterol 35mg		**11**%
Sodium 490mg		**20**%
Total Carbohydrate 33g		**11**%
Dietary Fiber 6g		**24**%
Sugars 2g		
Protein 17g		

Vitamin A 10%   Vitamin C 60%

Calcium 6%   Iron 15%

Food Exchanges
1 vegetable, 1½ starch, 1 meat

Middle Eastern Veggie
Serving Size: 1 sandwich

Amount per serving

Calories 280 Calories from fat 60

% Daily Value*

Total Fat 7g		**10**%
Saturated Fat 0g		**0**%
Cholesterol 0mg		**0**%
Sodium 540mg		**22**%
Total Carbohydrate 50g		**17**%
Dietary Fiber 10g		**39**%
Sugars 6g		
Protein 11g		

Vitamin A 160%   Vitamin C 60%

Calcium 6%   Iron 20%

Food Exchanges
2 vegetable, 2½ starch, 1 fat

Thai Tuna
Serving Size: 1 sandwich

Amount per serving

Calories 270 Calories from fat 60

% Daily Value*

Total Fat 7g		**10**%
Saturated Fat 1.5g		**7**%
Cholesterol 35mg		**12**%
Sodium 820mg		**34**%
Total Carbohydrate 28g		**9**%
Dietary Fiber 4g		**17**%
Sugars 3g		
Protein 26g		

Vitamin A 8%   Vitamin C 15%

Calcium 6%   Iron 15%

Food Exchanges
2 starch, 3 meat

Grains

Asian Rice
Serving Size: ⅔ cup

Amount per serving

Calories 170 Calories from fat 25

% Daily Value*

Total Fat 3g		**5**%
Saturated Fat 1g		**5**%
Sodium 77mg		**3**%
Total Carbohydrate 31g		**10**%
Dietary Fiber 1g		**4**%
Sugars 2g		
Protein 4g		

Vitamin A 28%   Vitamin C 3%

Calcium 3%   Iron 11%

Food Exchanges
2 starch, ½ fat

Italian Rice
Serving Size: ⅔ cup

Amount per serving

Calories 170 Calories from fat 25

% Daily Value*

Total Fat 3g		**5**%
Saturated Fat 1g		**5**%
Sodium 45mg		**2**%
Total Carbohydrate 31g		**10**%
Dietary Fiber 1g		**4**%
Sugars 1g		
Protein 4g		

Vitamin A 0%   Vitamin C 15%

Calcium 3%   Iron 7%

Food Exchanges
2 starch, ½ fat

Mexican Rice
Serving Size: ¾ cup

Amount per serving

Calories 180 Calories from fat 20

% Daily Value*

Total Fat 2g		**3**%
Saturated Fat 1g		**5**%
Sodium 18mg		**1**%
Total Carbohydrate 35g		**12**%
Dietary Fiber 2g		**8**%
Sugars 1g		
Protein 5g		

Vitamin A 5%   Vitamin C 4%

Calcium 4%   Iron 10%

Food Exchanges
2 starch

Moroccan Couscous
Serving Size: ⅔ cup

Amount per serving

Calories 170 Calories from fat 25

% Daily Value*

Total Fat 3g		**3**%
Saturated Fat 0g		**0**%
Sodium 50mg		**2**%
Total Carbohydrate 30g		**10**%
Dietary Fiber 6g		**25**%
Sugars 4g		
Protein 5g		

Vitamin A 0%   Vitamin C 10%

Calcium 3%   Iron 6%

Food Exchanges
2 starch, ½ fat

Southwestern Quinoa
Serving Size: ⅔ cup

Amount per serving

Calories 160 Calories from fat 45

% Daily Value*

Total Fat 5g		**8**%
Saturated Fat 1g		**5**%
Sodium 20mg		**1**%
Total Carbohydrate 24g		**8**%
Dietary Fiber 2g		**8**%
Sugars 1g		
Protein 5g		

Vitamin A 6%   Vitamin C 4%

Calcium 4%   Iron 18%

Food Exchanges
1½ starch, 1 fat

Veggies

Asian Carrots
Serving Size: 1 cup

Amount per serving

Calories 90 Calories from fat 25

% Daily Value*

Total Fat 3g		**5**%
Saturated Fat 0g		**0**%
Sodium 40mg		**2**%
Total Carbohydrate 12g		**4**%
Dietary Fiber 5g		**20**%
Sugars 7g		
Protein 1g		

Vitamin A 200%   Vitamin C 15%

Calcium 2%   Iron 6%

Food Exchanges
2 vegetable, ½ fat

Mediterranean Broccoli
Serving Size: ¾ cup

Amount per serving

Calories 40 Calories from fat 15

% Daily Value*

Total Fat 1.5g		**2**%
Saturated Fat 0g		**0**%
Sodium 25mg		**1**%
Total Carbohydrate 5g		**2**%
Dietary Fiber 3g		**11**%
Sugars 2g		
Protein 3g		

Vitamin A 25%   Vitamin C 130%

Calcium 4%   Iron 4%

Food Exchanges
1 vegetable

Italian Zucchini
Serving Size: 1 cup

Amount per serving

Calories 45 Calories from fat 20

% Daily Value*

Total Fat 2g		**3**%
Saturated Fat 0g		**0**%
Sodium 10mg		**0**%
Total Carbohydrate 6g		**2**%
Dietary Fiber 2g		**8**%
Sugars 4g		
Protein 2g		

Vitamin A 90%   Vitamin C 25%

Calcium 2%   Iron 4%

Food Exchanges
1 vegetable, ½ fat

Mexican Peppers & Onions
Serving Size: 1 cup

Amount per serving

Calories 70 Calories from fat 25

% Daily Value*

Total Fat 3g		**5**%
Saturated Fat 0g		**0**%
Sodium 0mg		**0**%
Total Carbohydrate 11g		**4**%
Dietary Fiber 3g		**12**%
Sugars 5g		
Protein 1g		

Vitamin A 80%   Vitamin C 280%

Calcium 2%   Iron 4%

Food Exchanges
2 vegetable, ½ fat

Irish Green Beans
Serving Size: 1 cup

Amount per serving

Calories 45 Calories from fat 0

% Daily Value*

Total Fat 0g		**0**%
Saturated Fat 0g		**0**%
Sodium 10mg		**0**%
Total Carbohydrate 9g		**3**%
Dietary Fiber 4g		**12**%
Sugars 5g		
Protein 2g		

Vitamin A 8%   Vitamin C 25%

Calcium 6%   Iron 2%

Food Exchanges
2 vegetable

Chicken, Fish, & Soy

Asian Tofu
Serving Size: 3.2 oz

Amount per serving

Calories 110 Calories from fat 50

	% Daily Value*
Total Fat 6g	**9%**
Saturated Fat 1g	**5%**
Sodium 220mg	**9%**
Total Carbohydrate 4g	**1%**
Dietary Fiber 2g	**8%**
Protein 9g	

Vitamin A 0%	Vitamin C 0%
Calcium 4%	Iron 8%

Food Exchanges
2 meat, 1 fat

Cajun Chicken
Serving Size: 3 oz

Amount per serving

Calories 130 Calories from fat 50

	% Daily Value*
Total Fat 5g	**8%**
Saturated Fat 1.5g	**8%**
Cholesterol 70mg	**23%**
Sodium 240mg	**10%**
Total Carbohydrate 2g	**1%**
Protein 16g	

Vitamin A 2%	Vitamin C 4%
Calcium 0%	Iron 4%

Food Exchanges
3 lean meat

Cuban Fish
Serving Size: 3 oz

Amount per serving

Calories 90 Calories from fat 15

	% Daily Value*
Total Fat 1.5g	**2%**
Saturated Fat 1g	**5%**
Sodium 90mg	**4%**
Total Carbohydrate 2g	**1%**
Protein 18g	

Vitamin A 2%	Vitamin C 6%
Calcium 4%	Iron 2%

Food Exchanges
3 lean meat

French Salmon
Serving Size: 3 oz

Amount per serving

Calories 120 Calories from fat 35

	% Daily Value*
Total Fat 4g	**6%**
Saturated Fat 1.5g	**8%**
Cholesterol 55mg	**18%**
Sodium 70mg	**3%**
Total Carbohydrate 0g	**0%**
Protein 21g	

Vitamin A 4%	Vitamin C 0%
Calcium 0%	Iron 4%

Food Exchanges
3 meat

Mediterranean Chicken
Serving Size: 3 oz

Amount per serving

Calories 120 Calories from fat 25

	% Daily Value*
Total Fat 2.5g	**4%**
Saturated Fat 0g	**0%**
Cholesterol 55mg	**18%**
Sodium 110mg	**5%**
Total Carbohydrate 2g	**1%**
Protein 21g	

Vitamin A 0%	Vitamin C 4%
Calcium 0%	Iron 4%

Food Exchanges
3 lean meat

Pizza

Asian
Serving Size: 1/5 pizza

Amount per serving

Calories 330 Calories from fat 25

	% Daily Value*
Total Fat 3g	**5%**
Saturated Fat .5g	**2%**
Cholesterol 0mg	**0%**
Sodium 590mg	**25%**
Total Carbohydrate 65g	**22%**
Dietary Fiber 3g	**12%**
Sugars 8g	
Protein 14g	

Vitamin A 8%	Vitamin C 100%
Calcium 10%	Iron 30%

Food Exchanges
2 vegetable, 3 starch, 1 fat

Greek
Serving Size: 1/5 pizza

Amount per serving

Calories 330 Calories from fat 40

	% Daily Value*
Total Fat 5g	**8%**
Saturated Fat .5g	**2%**
Cholesterol 0mg	**0%**
Sodium 320mg	**13%**
Total Carbohydrate 63g	**21%**
Dietary Fiber 2g	**8%**
Sugars 15g	
Protein 10g	

Vitamin A 15%	Vitamin C 70%
Calcium 8%	Iron 20%

Food Exchanges
1 fruit, 3 starch, 1 fat

Italian
Serving Size: 1/5 pizza

Amount per serving

Calories 360 Calories from fat 40

	% Daily Value*
Total Fat 4g	**6%**
Saturated Fat .5g	**2%**
Cholesterol 10mg	**3%**
Sodium 800mg	**30%**
Total Carbohydrate 66g	**22%**
Dietary Fiber 4g	**16%**
Sugars 6g	
Protein 19g	

Vitamin A 130%	Vitamin C 30%
Calcium 8%	Iron 25%

Food Exchanges
3 vegetable, 3 starch, 1 fat

Mediterranean
Serving Size: 1/5 pizza

Amount per serving

Calories 320 Calories from fat 60

	% Daily Value*
Total Fat 6g	**9%**
Saturated Fat 1.5g	**8%**
Cholesterol 5mg	**2%**
Sodium 500mg	**21%**
Total Carbohydrate 55g	**18%**
Dietary Fiber 2g	**8%**
Sugars 6g	
Protein 13g	

Vitamin A 8%	Vitamin C 25%
Calcium 15%	Iron 20%

Food Exchanges
1 vegetable, 3 starch, 1 fat

Mexican
Serving Size: 1/5 pizza

Amount per serving

Calories 270 Calories from fat 60

	% Daily Value*
Total Fat 7g	**11%**
Saturated Fat 2.5g	**12%**
Cholesterol 15mg	**5%**
Sodium 800mg	**30%**
Total Carbohydrate 41g	**14%**
Dietary Fiber 5g	**20%**
Sugars 3g	
Protein 13g	

Vitamin A 15%	Vitamin C 150%
Calcium 25%	Iron 20%

Food Exchanges
1 vegetable, 2 starch, 1 meat, 1 fat

Stews

Southwestern Corn
Serving Size: about 2 cups

Amount per serving

Calories 280 Calories from fat 60

	% Daily Value*
Total Fat 7g	**11%**
Saturated Fat 1.5g	**8%**
Cholesterol 5mg	**2%**
Sodium 160mg	**7%**
Total Carbohydrate 43g	**14%**
Dietary Fiber 6g	**23%**
Sugars 6g	
Protein 18g	

Vitamin A 15%	Vitamin C 45%
Calcium 15%	Iron 20%

Food Exchanges
2 vegetable, 2 starch, 1 lean meat, 1 fat

Mexican Bean
Serving Size: about 2 cups

Amount per serving

Calories 250 Calories from fat 45

	% Daily Value*
Total Fat 5g	**8%**
Saturated Fat 1g	**5%**
Cholesterol 0mg	**0%**
Sodium 380mg	**16%**
Total Carbohydrate 44g	**15%**
Dietary Fiber 13g	**53%**
Sugars 12g	
Protein 12g	

Vitamin A 250%	Vitamin C 150%
Calcium 15%	Iron 20%

Food Exchanges
5 vegetable, 1 starch, 1 lean meat, 1/2 fat

Moroccan Vegetable
Serving Size: about 1 3/4 cups

Amount per serving

Calories 200 Calories from fat 50

	% Daily Value*
Total Fat 6g	**9%**
Saturated Fat 0.5g	**3%**
Cholesterol 0mg	**0%**
Sodium 250mg	**10%**
Total Carbohydrate 33g	**11%**
Dietary Fiber 10g	**42%**
Sugars 11g	
Protein 7g	

Vitamin A 450%	Vitamin C 110%
Calcium 10%	Iron 15%

Food Exchanges
3 vegetable, 1 starch, 1 fat

Creole Fish
Serving Size: about 1 3/4 cups

Amount per serving

Calories 260 Calories from fat 50

	% Daily Value*
Total Fat 5g	**9%**
Saturated Fat 1.5g	**7%**
Cholesterol 40mg	**13%**
Sodium 190mg	**8%**
Total Carbohydrate 31g	**10%**
Dietary Fiber 3g	**11%**
Sugars 7g	
Protein 22g	

Vitamin A 15%	Vitamin C 80%
Calcium 6%	Iron 10%

Food Exchanges
2 vegetable, 1 starch, 3 lean meat

African Sweet Potato
Serving Size: about 1 3/4 cups

Amount per serving

Calories 320 Calories from fat 90

	% Daily Value*
Total Fat 10g	**16%**
Saturated Fat 1.5g	**7%**
Cholesterol 0mg	**0%**
Sodium 85mg	**3%**
Total Carbohydrate 52g	**17%**
Dietary Fiber 9g	**36%**
Sugars 23g	
Protein 9g	

Vitamin A 470%	Vitamin C 130%
Calcium 10%	Iron 15%

Food Exchanges
4 vegetable, 2 starch, 2 fat

Pasta

Asian
Serving Size: 1½ cups

Amount per serving

Calories 300 Calories from fat 45

% Daily Value*

Total Fat 5g	**8%**
Saturated Fat .5g	**3%**
Cholesterol 20mg	**7%**
Sodium 420mg	**18%**
Total Carbohydrate 46g	**15%**
Dietary Fiber 4g	**12%**
Sugars 4g	
Protein 17g	

Vitamin A 120%	Vitamin C 40%
Calcium 6%	Iron 20%

Food Exchanges
1 vegetable, 3 starch,
1 lean meat

French
Serving Size: 1½ cups

Amount per serving

Calories 420 Calories from fat 20

% Daily Value*

Total Fat 2g	**3%**
Saturated Fat .5g	**2%**
Cholesterol 25mg	**8%**
Sodium 370mg	**15%**
Total Carbohydrate 66g	**22%**
Dietary Fiber 2g	**8%**
Sugars 7g	
Protein 27g	

Vitamin A 15%	Vitamin C 35%
Calcium 25%	Iron 35%

Food Exchanges
3 vegetable, 3½ starch,
1 lean meat

Italian
Serving Size: 1½ cups

Amount per serving

Calories 310 Calories from fat 35

% Daily Value*

Total Fat 4g	**6%**
Saturated Fat .5g	**2%**
Cholesterol 0mg	**0%**
Sodium 125mg	**15%**
Total Carbohydrate 54g	**18%**
Dietary Fiber 5g	**20%**
Sugars 7g	
Protein 11g	

Vitamin A 15%	Vitamin C 60%
Calcium 8%	Iron 35%

Food Exchanges
2 vegetable, 3 starch, 1 fat

Mexican
Serving Size: 1½ cups

Amount per serving

Calories 350 Calories from fat 35

% Daily Value*

Total Fat 4g	**6%**
Saturated Fat .5g	**2%**
Cholesterol 35mg	**12%**
Sodium 330mg	**14%**
Total Carbohydrate 56g	**19%**
Dietary Fiber 6g	**24%**
Sugars 6g	
Protein 22g	

Vitamin A 15%	Vitamin C 70%
Calcium 8%	Iron 40%

Food Exchanges
2 vegetable, 3 starch,
1 lean mean, ½ fat

Spanish
Serving Size: 1½ cups

Amount per serving

Calories 350 Calories from fat 35

% Daily Value*

Total Fat 4g	**6%**
Saturated Fat .5g	**2%**
Cholesterol 15mg	**5%**
Sodium 65mg	**3%**
Total Carbohydrate 57g	**19%**
Dietary Fiber 5g	**18%**
Sugars 7g	
Protein 18g	

Vitamin A 40%	Vitamin C 160%
Calcium 6%	Iron 25%

Food Exchanges
3 vegetable, 3 starch,
1 lean meat

More Pasta

Japanese
Serving Size: 1½ cups

Amount per serving

Calories 260 Calories from fat 70

% Daily Value*

Total Fat 8g	**12%**
Saturated Fat 1g	**4%**
Cholesterol 0mg	**0%**
Sodium 760mg	**32%**
Total Carbohydrate 41g	**14%**
Dietary Fiber 2g	**9%**
Sugars 3g	
Protein 7g	

Vitamin A 160%	Vitamin C 25%
Calcium 4%	Iron 6%

Food Exchanges
1 vegetable, 2 starch, 1 fat

Greek
Serving Size: 1½ cups

Amount per serving

Calories 350 Calories from fat 60

% Daily Value*

Total Fat 7g	**10%**
Saturated Fat 2g	**10%**
Cholesterol 10mg	**3%**
Sodium 180mg	**7%**
Total Carbohydrate 55g	**18%**
Dietary Fiber 5g	**20%**
Sugars 7g	
Protein 20g	

Vitamin A 110%	Vitamin C 70%
Calcium 20%	Iron 30%

Food Exchanges
2 vegetable, 3 starch,
1 lean meat, 1 fat

Mediterranean
Serving Size: 1½ cups

Amount per serving

Calories 350 Calories from fat 60

% Daily Value*

Total Fat 6g	**8%**
Saturated Fat 1.5g	**9%**
Cholesterol 5mg	**1%**
Sodium 125mg	**5%**
Total Carbohydrate 55g	**18%**
Dietary Fiber 5g	**20%**
Sugars 7g	
Protein 20g	

Vitamin A 110%	Vitamin C 90%
Calcium 15%	Iron 25%

Food Exchanges
2 vegetable, 3 starch,
1 lean meat, 1 fat

Portuguese
Serving Size: 1½ cups

Amount per serving

Calories 350 Calories from fat 50

% Daily Value*

Total Fat 6g	**9%**
Saturated Fat 1g	**5%**
Cholesterol 30mg	**10%**
Sodium 350mg	**15%**
Total Carbohydrate 47g	**18%**
Dietary Fiber 3g	**14%**
Sugars 4g	
Protein 29g	

Vitamin A 6%	Vitamin C 10%
Calcium 8%	Iron 30%

Food Exchanges
2 vegetable, 2½ starch,
3 lean meat

Southwestern Mole
Serving Size: 1½ cups

Amount per serving

Calories 370 Calories from fat 60

% Daily Value*

Total Fat 7g	**11%**
Saturated Fat 1.5g	**7%**
Cholesterol 60mg	**19%**
Sodium 65mg	**3%**
Total Carbohydrate 43g	**14%**
Dietary Fiber 3g	**13%**
Sugars 5g	
Protein 35g	

Vitamin A 10%	Vitamin C 30%
Calcium 6%	Iron 25%

Food Exchanges
1 vegetable, 2½ starch,
3 lean meat, 1 fat

Sauté

Asian
Serving Size: 1½ cups

Amount per serving

Calories 280 Calories from fat 40

% Daily Value*

Total Fat 4g	**6%**
Saturated Fat .5g	**2%**
Cholesterol 10mg	**3%**
Sodium 320mg	**13%**
Total Carbohydrate 51g	**17%**
Dietary Fiber 5g	**20%**
Sugars 9g	
Protein 14g	

Vitamin A 240%	Vitamin C 80%
Calcium 8%	Iron 15%

Food Exchanges
2 vegetable, 2½ starch, 1 meat

Indian
Serving Size: 1½ cups

Amount per serving

Calories 317 Calories from fat 47

% Daily Value*

Total Fat 5g	**10%**
Saturated Fat 0g	**2%**
Sodium 137mg	**5%**
Total Carbohydrate 63g	**20%**
Dietary Fiber 5g	**20%**
Sugars 9g	
Protein 7g	

Vitamin A 240%	Vitamin C 25%
Calcium 8%	Iron 10%

Food Exchanges
4 starch, 1 fat

Indonesian
Serving Size: 1½ cups

Amount per serving

Calories 290 Calories from fat 45

% Daily Value*

Total Fat 5g	**8%**
Saturated Fat 1g	**5%**
Sodium 270mg	**11%**
Total Carbohydrate 53g	**18%**
Dietary Fiber 5g	**20%**
Sugars 12g	
Protein 9g	

Vitamin A 25%	Vitamin C 70%
Calcium 10%	Iron 20%

Food Exchanges
2 vegetable, 2½ starch, 1 fat

Mexican
Serving Size: 1½ cups

Amount per serving

Calories 300 Calories from fat 60

% Daily Value*

Total Fat 6g	**9%**
Saturated Fat .5g	**2%**
Sodium 300mg	**12%**
Total Carbohydrate 57g	**19%**
Dietary Fiber 7g	**28%**
Sugars 6g	
Protein 10g	

Vitamin A 8%	Vitamin C 220%
Calcium 8%	Iron 20%

Food Exchanges
3 vegetable, 2½ starch, 1 fat

Moroccan
Serving Size: 1½ cups

Amount per serving

Calories 270 Calories from fat 20

% Daily Value*

Total Fat 2g	**3%**
Saturated Fat .5g	**2%**
Cholesterol 25mg	**8%**
Sodium 200mg	**8%**
Total Carbohydrate 46g	**15%**
Dietary Fiber 11g	**44%**
Sugars 6g	
Protein 18g	

Vitamin A 8%	Vitamin C 130%
Calcium 8%	Iron 10%

Food Exchanges
2 vegetable, 2½ starch, 1 meat

Stir-Fry

Indian
Serving Size: 1½ cups

Amount per serving

Calories 180 Calories from fat 60

% Daily Value*

Total Fat 7g	**11**%
Saturated Fat .5g	**2**%
Cholesterol 0mg	**0**%
Sodium 20mg	**1**%
Total Carbohydrate 43g	**18**%
Dietary Fiber 2g	**8**%
Sugars 5g	
Protein 8g	

Vitamin A 20%   Vitamin C 160%

Calcium 15%   Iron 20%

Food Exchanges
1 vegetable, 2½ starch, 1 fat

Italian
Serving Size: 2 cups

Amount per serving

Calories 310 Calories from fat 60

% Daily Value*

Total Fat 6g	**9**%
Saturated Fat 1g	**10**%
Cholesterol 5mg	**2**%
Sodium 210mg	**9**%
Total Carbohydrate 53g	**18**%
Dietary Fiber 5g	**20**%
Sugars 5g	
Protein 15g	

Vitamin A 25%   Vitamin C 80%

Calcium 15%   Iron 25%

Food Exchanges
1 vegetable, 3 starch, 1 fat

Japanese
Serving Size: 2 cups

Amount per serving

Calories 290 Calories from fat 50

% Daily Value*

Total Fat 6g	**9**%
Saturated Fat 1g	**5**%
Cholesterol 0mg	**0**%
Sodium 150mg	**6**%
Total Carbohydrate 52g	**17**%
Dietary Fiber 5g	**20**%
Sugars 5g	
Protein 13g	

Vitamin A 15%   Vitamin C 140%

Calcium 8%   Iron 25%

Food Exchanges
1 vegetable, 3 starch, 1 fat

Mexican
Serving Size: 1½ cups

Amount per serving

Calories 180 Calories from fat 60

% Daily Value*

Total Fat 7g	**11**%
Saturated Fat .5g	**2**%
Cholesterol 0mg	**0**%
Sodium 460mg	**19**%
Total Carbohydrate 45g	**15**%
Dietary Fiber 7g	**28**%
Sugars 4g	
Protein 9g	

Vitamin A 120%   Vitamin C 60%

Calcium 8%   Iron 15%

Food Exchanges
2 vegetable, 2 starch, 1 fat

Thai
Serving Size: 1½ cups

Amount per serving

Calories 250 Calories from fat 50

% Daily Value*

Total Fat 5g	**8**%
Saturated Fat 1g	**5**%
Cholesterol 0mg	**0**%
Sodium 680mg	**28**%
Total Carbohydrate 49g	**16**%
Dietary Fiber 5g	**20**%
Sugars 7g	
Protein 7g	

Vitamin A 120%   Vitamin C 90%

Calcium 15%   Iron 20%

Food Exchanges
2 vegetable, 2 starch, 1 fat

More Stir-Fry

Latin
Serving Size: about 1¼ cups

Amount per serving

Calories 230 Calories from fat 50

% Daily Value*

Total Fat 6g	**9**%
Saturated Fat 1g	**6**%
Cholesterol 60mg	**19**%
Sodium 190mg	**8**%
Total Carbohydrate 25g	**8**%
Dietary Fiber 4g	**15**%
Sugars 5g	
Protein 25g	

Vitamin A 50%   Vitamin C 160%

Calcium 4%   Iron 10%

Food Exchanges
2 vegetable, 1 starch
3 lean meat, 1 fat

Hawaiian
Serving Size: about 1¼ cups

Amount per serving

Calories 260 Calories from fat 40

% Daily Value*

Total Fat 4.5g	**7**%
Saturated Fat 0g	**0**%
Cholesterol 30mg	**10**%
Sodium 170mg	**7**%
Total Carbohydrate 40g	**13**%
Dietary Fiber 5g	**20**%
Sugars 8g	
Protein 17g	

Vitamin A 300%   Vitamin C 80%

Calcium 8%   Iron 10%

Food Exchanges
2 vegetable, 2 starch,
2 meat, ½ fat

Pan Asian
Serving Size: about 1½ cups

Amount per serving

Calories 320 Calories from fat 60

% Daily Value*

Total Fat 7g	**10**%
Saturated Fat 1g	**5**%
Cholesterol 60mg	**19**%
Sodium 240mg	**10**%
Total Carbohydrate 40g	**13**%
Dietary Fiber 7g	**27**%
Sugars 6g	
Protein 28g	

Vitamin A 180%   Vitamin C 70%

Calcium 20%   Iron 30%

Food Exchanges
2 vegetable, 2 starch,
3 lean meat, ½ fat

Caribbean
Serving Size: about 1½ cups

Amount per serving

Calories 360 Calories from fat 80

% Daily Value*

Total Fat 8g	**13**%
Saturated Fat 1.5g	**6**%
Cholesterol 60mg	**19**%
Sodium 90mg	**4**%
Total Carbohydrate 45g	**15**%
Dietary Fiber 5g	**21**%
Sugars 10g	
Protein 28g	

Vitamin A 150%   Vitamin C 210%

Calcium 15%   Iron 15%

Food Exchanges
4 vegetable, 1½ starch,
3 lean meat, 1 fat

Indonesian
Serving Size: about 2 cups

Amount per serving

Calories 380 Calories from fat 80

% Daily Value*

Total Fat 9g	**14**%
Saturated Fat 1.5g	**7**%
Cholesterol 60mg	**19**%
Sodium 420mg	**17**%
Total Carbohydrate 47g	**16**%
Dietary Fiber 10g	**39**%
Sugars 9g	
Protein 29g	

Vitamin A 310%   Vitamin C 140%

Calcium 15%   Iron 15%

Food Exchanges
4 vegetable, 1½ starch,
3 meat, 1 fat

Oven-Baked

French
Serving Size: ⅕ recipe

Amount per serving

Calories 230 Calories from fat 45

% Daily Value*

Total Fat 5g	**8**%
Saturated Fat 3g	**15**%
Cholesterol 10mg	**3**%
Sodium 300mg	**12**%
Total Carbohydrate 34g	**11**%
Dietary Fiber 5g	**20**%
Sugars 8g	
Protein 11g	

Vitamin A 15%   Vitamin C 90%

Calcium 30%   Iron 10%

Food Exchanges
2 vegetable, 1½ starch, 1 fat

Spanish
Serving Size: ⅕ recipe

Amount per serving

Calories 350 Calories from fat 50

% Daily Value*

Total Fat 6g	**9**%
Saturated Fat 1.5g	**7**%
Cholesterol 30mg	**10**%
Sodium 135mg	**6**%
Total Carbohydrate 49g	**16**%
Dietary Fiber 3g	**13**%
Sugars 9g	
Protein 24g	

Vitamin A 150%   Vitamin C 50%

Calcium 15%   Iron 20%

Food Exchanges
3 vegetable, 2 starch,
3 lean meat

Italian
Serving Size: ⅕ recipe

Amount per serving

Calories 260 Calories from fat 45

% Daily Value*

Total Fat 5g	**8**%
Saturated Fat .5g	**2**%
Cholesterol 10mg	**3**%
Sodium 180mg	**8**%
Total Carbohydrate 42g	**14**%
Dietary Fiber 5g	**20**%
Sugars 3g	
Protein 13g	

Vitamin A 30%   Vitamin C 80%

Calcium 20%   Iron 25%

Food Exchanges
3 vegetable, 1 starch, 1 meat,
1 fat

Mediterranean
Serving Size: ⅕ recipe

Amount per serving

Calories 280 Calories from fat 90

% Daily Value*

Total Fat 9g	**13**%
Saturated Fat 4.5g	**22**%
Cholesterol 25mg	**8**%
Sodium 710mg	**30**%
Total Carbohydrate 41g	**14**%
Dietary Fiber 7g	**28**%
Sugars 4g	
Protein 12g	

Vitamin A 70%   Vitamin C 60%

Calcium 30%   Iron 20%

Food Exchanges
2 vegetable, 2 starch, 2 fat

Mexican
Serving Size: ⅕ recipe

Amount per serving

Calories 280 Calories from fat 60

% Daily Value*

Total Fat 7g	**11**%
Saturated Fat 1.5g	**8**%
Cholesterol 10mg	**3**%
Sodium 600mg	**25**%
Total Carbohydrate 39g	**13**%
Dietary Fiber 7g	**28**%
Sugars 3g	
Protein 12g	

Vitamin A 15%   Vitamin C 170%

Calcium 30%   Iron 10%

Food Exchanges
1 vegetable, 2 starch, 1 meat,
1 fat

Desserts

Hawaiian Medley

Serving Size: 1 cup

Amount per serving

Calories 130 Calories from fat 15

	% Daily Value*
Total Fat 1.5g	**2**%
Saturated Fat 0g	**0**%
Sodium 0mg	**0**%
Total Carbohydrate 31g	**10**%
Dietary Fiber 3g	**12**%
Sugars 25g	
Protein 2g	

Vitamin A 4%	Vitamin C 25%
Calcium 2%	Iron 4%

Food Exchanges

2 fruit

Italian Bella Frutta

Serving Size: 1 cup

Amount per serving

Calories 100 Calories from fat 15

	% Daily Value*
Total Fat 1g	**2**%
Saturated Fat 0g	**0**%
Sodium 0mg	**0**%
Total Carbohydrate 23g	**8**%
Dietary Fiber 3g	**12**%
Sugars 17g	
Protein 1g	

Vitamin A 0%	Vitamin C 15%
Calcium 0%	Iron 4%

Food Exchanges

1½ fruit

French Citrus Supreme

Serving Size: 1 cup

Amount per serving

Calories 70 Calories from fat 10

	% Daily Value*
Total Fat 1g	**2**%
Saturated Fat 0g	**0**%
Sodium 0mg	**0**%
Total Carbohydrate 18g	**6**%
Dietary Fiber 5g	**18**%
Sugars 13g	
Protein 2g	

Vitamin A 0%	Vitamin C 130%
Calcium 6%	Iron 4%

Food Exchanges

1 fruit

American Apple Berry

Serving Size: 1 cup

Amount per serving

Calories 130 Calories from fat 15

	% Daily Value*
Total Fat 1.5g	**2**%
Saturated Fat .5g	**2**%
Sodium 15mg	**1**%
Total Carbohydrate 28g	**9**%
Dietary Fiber 4g	**16**%
Sugars 14g	
Protein 1g	

Vitamin A 2%	Vitamin C 80%
Calcium 4%	Iron 4%

Food Exchanges

2 fruit

New Zealand Delight

Serving Size: 1 cup

Amount per serving

Calories 90 Calories from fat 15

	% Daily Value*
Total Fat 1g	**1**%
Saturated Fat 0g	**0**%
Sodium 5mg	**0**%
Total Carbohydrate 20g	**7**%
Dietary Fiber 5g	**20**%
Sugars 15g	
Protein 2g	

Vitamin A 0%	Vitamin C 170%
Calcium 8%	Iron 6%

Food Exchanges

1½ fruit

Food & Nutrition Resources

Associations

American Diabetes Association
1701 North Beauregard St.
Alexandria, VA 22311
1-800-342-2383
www.diabetes.org

The American Dietetic Association
216 W. Jackson Blvd., Suite 800
Chicago, IL 60606-6995
1-800-366-1635
www.eatright.org (has links to other health and nutrition websites)

5 A Day
www.5aday.com

Newsletters

Environmental Nutrition
P.O. Box 420451
Palm Coast, FL 32142-0451
800-829-5384

Nutrition Action Health Letter
Center for Science in the Public Interest
1875 Connecticut Ave., N.W., Suite 300
Washington, D.C. 20009-5728
www.cspinet.org (has links to other health and nutrition websites)

Tufts University Health & Nutrition Letter
P.O. Box 57857
Boulder, CO 80322-7857
1-800-274-7581
www.healthletter.tufts.edu (has links to other health and nutrition websites)

University of California, Berkeley Wellness Letter
P.O. Box 420148
Palm Coast, FL 32142
800-829-9170

About the American Diabetes Association

The American Diabetes Association is the nation's leading voluntary health organization supporting diabetes research, information, and advocacy. Its mission is to prevent and cure diabetes and to improve the lives of all people affected by diabetes. The American Diabetes Association is the leading publisher of comprehensive diabetes information. Its huge library of practical and authoritative books for people with diabetes covers every aspect of self-care—cooking and nutrition, fitness, weight control, medications, complications, emotional issues, and general self-care.

To order American Diabetes Association books: Call 1-800-232-6733. http://store.diabetes.org [Note: there is no need to use **www** when typing this particular Web address]

To join the American Diabetes Association: Call 1-800-806-7801. www.diabetes.org/membership

For more information about diabetes or ADA programs and services: Call 1-800-342-2383. E-mail: Customerservice@diabetes.org www.diabetes.org

To locate an ADA/NCQA Recognized Provider of quality diabetes care in your area: Call 1-703-549-1500 ext. 2202. www.diabetes.org/recognition/Physicians/ListAll.asp

To find an ADA Recognized Education Program in your area: Call 1-888-232-0822. www.diabetes.org/recognition/education.asp

To join the fight to increase funding for diabetes research, end discrimination, and improve insurance coverage: Call 1-800-342-2383. www.diabetes.org/advocacy

To find out how you can get involved with the programs in your community: Call 1-800-342-2383. See below for program Web addresses.

- *American Diabetes Month:* Educational activities aimed at those diagnosed with diabetes—month of November. www.diabetes.org/ADM

- *American Diabetes Alert:* Annual public awareness campaign to find the undiagnosed—held the fourth Tuesday in March. www.diabetes.org/alert

- *The Diabetes Assistance & Resources Program (DAR):* diabetes awareness program targeted to the Latino community. www.diabetes.org/DAR

- *African American Program:* diabetes awareness program targeted to the African American community. www.diabetes.org/africanamerican

- *Awakening the Spirit: Pathways to Diabetes Prevention & Control:* diabetes awareness program targeted to the Native American community. www.diabetes.org/awakening

To find out about an important research project regarding type 2 diabetes: www.diabetes.org/ada/research.asp

To obtain information on making a planned gift or charitable bequest: Call 1-888-700-7029. www.diabetes.org/ada/plan.asp

To make a donation or memorial contribution: Call 1-800-342-2383. www.diabetes.org/ada/cont.asp